To L. V. B.

LITERARY IMPRESSIONISM

by

Maria Elisabeth Kronegger

College & University Press · *Publishers*

NEW HAVEN, CONN.

Library of Congress Catalog Card Number: 72-79803

MANUFACTURED IN THE UNITED STATES OF AMERICA BY
UNITED PRINTING SERVICES, INC.
NEW HAVEN, CONN.

Literary Impressionism

Acknowledgments

I wish to express my gratitude to the Ford Foundation and to the All University Research Fund of Michigan State University for both funds and time provided to prepare the manuscript for publication.

I am most grateful to Professor Laurence M. Porter whose perceptive suggestions have substantially improved this study. Finally, I acknowledge a deep gratitude to Mrs. Jeanne Sundström and Professor Eugene Gray who generously helped me in translating certain passages from German and French into English.

Grateful acknowledgment is made to the following publishers for permission to quote from their publications: Albin Michel for René Albérès, *L'Aventure Intellectuelle du XXe siècle* (1959), *Histoire du Roman Moderne* (1962), *Métamorphoses du Roman* (1966), *Le Roman d'Aujourd'hui 1960-70* (1970) and John Rewald, *Cézanne* (1939); Cambridge University Press for Stephen Ullmann, *Style in the French Novel* (1957); Chatto and Windus for Marcel Proust, *Remembrance of Things Past*, "Time Regained," vol. XII, tr. Andreas Mayor (1970); Armand Colin for Pierre Henri Simon, *Théâtre Destin* (1959); Delphin Verlag for Hermann Bahr, *Expressionismus* (1918); J. M. Dent & Sons for Joseph Conrad, *The Nigger of the "Narcissus"* (1897); Dodd, Mead & Co. for Camille Mauclair, *Monet* (1924); Doubleday Anchor Books for Ortega y Gasset, *The Dehumanization of Art* (1956); Droz for Emile Zola, *Salons* (1959); *Le Figaro Littéraire* for "Claude Simon, franc-tireur de la révolution romanesque" (April 6, 1967); Gallimard, Le Livre de Poche for André Gide, *Les Faux Monnayeurs* (1925), *Les Nourritures Terrestres* (1917-36), Marcel Proust, *Le Temps Retrouvé* (1954), Jean-Paul Sartre, *La Mort dans l'Ame* (1949), *La Nausée* (1938); Gallimard, NRF for André Gide, *Les Cahiers et les Poésies d'André Walter* (1952), Stéphane Mallarmé, *Correspondance 1862-1871*, ed. Henri Mondor (1959), Marcel Proust, *Oeuvres Complètes* (1919-24), Pierre Francastel,

Peinture et Société (1965), Alain Robbe-Grillet, *Pour le Nouveau Roman* (1963); Gallimard, Pleïade for Charles Baudelaire, *Oeuvres Complètes* (1954); Garnier Frères for Honoré de Balzac, *Le Lys dans la Vallée* (1966), Gustave Flaubert, *L'Education Sentimentale* (1964), Rimbaud, *Oeuvres* (1960); Harper & Row for *The Works of Honoré Balzac,* "The Lily of the Valley," n.d.; Max Hüber Verlag for Leo Spitzer, *Stilstudien* (1961); Inselverlag for Rainer Maria Rilke, *Sämtliche Werke,* "Die Aufzeichnungen des Malte Laurids Brigge" (1966); Alfred A. Knopf for André Gide, *The Counterfeiters* (1959), *The Fruits of Earth* (1957), *The Journals of André Gide,* vol. I, 1889-1913, tr. Justin O'Brien (1947), J.-P. Sartre, *Troubled Sleep* (1964); Kohlhammer Verlag for Hermann Bahr, *Zur Überwindung des Naturalismus* (1968); Macmillan & Co., Ltd., for Rainer Maria Rilke, *Selected Letters 1902-26,* tr. R. F. C. Hull (1947); Massin et Cie. (Lévy) for Ferdinand Brunetière, *Le Roman Naturaliste* (1893); Mercure de France for Remy de Gourmont, *Couleurs* (1920), Jules Laforgue, *Oeuvres Complètes,* "Mélanges Posthumes" (1903); Editions de Minuit for Claude Simon, *L'Herbe* (1958); Modern Library for Marcel Proust, *Swann's Way* (1948); Mouton & Co. for *Entretiens sur Marcel Proust* (1966); The Museum of Modern Art for John Rewald, *The History of Impressionism* (1961); Editions Nagel for Maurice Merleau-Ponty, *Sens et Non-Sens* (1948); New Directions for Jean-Paul Sartre, *Nausea* (1964); The University of Nebraska Press for *Literary Criticism of E. Poe,* ed. Robert L. Hough (1965); Northwestern University Press for Maurice Merleau-Ponty, "The Problem of Speech," *Themes from the Lectures at the Collège de France 1952-60* (1970); W. W. Norton & Co. for *Letters of Rainer Maria Rilke, 1892-1910,* tr. Jane Bannard Greene and M. D. Herter Norton (1945); Oxford University Press for Helmut A. Hatzfeld, *Literature through Art* (1952), Harry Levin, *The Gates of Horn* (1966); The Philosophical Library for Jean-Paul Sartre, *Being and Nothingness* (1948) and Lionello Venturi, "The Aesthetic Idea of Impressionism," *The Journal of Aesthetics and Art Criticism* (Spring 1941); Poligraphischer Verlag for Hugo Sommerhalder, *Zum Begriff des Literarischen Impressionismus* (1961); Prentice-Hall for *Flaubert,* a collection of critical essays, ed. Raymond Giraud (1964); Princeton University Press for Pierre Francastel, "La Fin de l'Impressionnisme: Esthétique et Causalité," in *Problems of the*

19th and 20th Studies in Western Art, IV (1963); Random House for Anna Balakian, *The Symbolist Movement* (1967); *Revue de Paris* for René Albérès, "Aux sources du nouveau roman: L'impressionnisme anglais," LXIX (May, 1962); Scribner's Sons for Lionello Venturi, *Painting and Painters* (1945); Editions du Seuil for Jean-Pierre Richard, *Littérature et Sensation* (1954); *La Table Ronde* for Pierre Decaves, "Réalités du Roman," 157 (Janvier, 1961); Universe Books, Inc., for Maurice Serullaz, *French Painting, the Impressionist Painters* (1960), The Viking Press for Roger Martin du Gard, *Recollections of André Gide* (1953); Vintage Books for Arnold Hauser, *The Social History of Art* (1960); The University of Wisconsin Press for Eugene F. Kaelin, *An Existentialist Aesthetic, the Theories of Sartre and Merleau-Ponty* (1966). Special acknowledgment is made to the Service Photographique de la Réunion des Musées Nationaux in Paris to use the following illustrations:

Eugène Delacroix, "Cheval attaqué par une Lionne," 1844; James McNeill Whistler, "Portrait of the Artist's Mother; Arrangement in Grey and Black," 1872; Camille Pissarro, "La diligence à Louveciennes," 1870; Pierre Auguste Renoir, "La Grenouillère," 1869; Claude Monet, "La Cathédrale de Rouen—plein soleil," 1894; "Femme à l'Ombrelle," 1886; and "Régates à Argenteuil," 1872; Edgar Degas, "Aux Courses: Jockeys amateurs près d'une voiture," 1879; Vincent Van Gogh, "L'Eglise d'Auvers," 1890; Paul Cézanne, "Nature Morte aux Oignons," 1888-90.

Translations

The Works of Honoré Balzac, with introductions by George Saintsbury, vol. IX. New York, London: Harper and Brothers, n.d., "The Lily of the Valley," pp. 89-92.

The Complete Works of Gustave Flaubert, with a critical introduction by Ferdinand Brunetière, *Sentimental Education.* vol. I, II. New York, London: M. Walter Dunne, 1904.

Gide, André. *The Counterfeiters.* New York: Alfred A. Knopf, 1959.

——. *The Fruits of Earth,* tr. Dorothy Bussy. New York: Alfred A. Knopf, 1957.

Proust, Marcel. *Swann's Way,* tr. C. K. Scott-Moncrieff. New York: Modern Library, 1948.

——. *Remembrance of Things Past,* "Time Regained," vol. XII, tr. Andreas Mayor. London: Chatto & Windus, 1970.

Rilke, Rainer Maria. *The Notebooks of Malte Laurids Brigge,* tr. M. D. Herter Norton. New York: W. W. Norton & Co., 1949.

Sartre, J.-P. *Nausea,* tr. Lloyd Alexander. New York: New Directions Paperback, 1964.

——. *Troubled Sleep,* tr. Gerard Hopkins. New York: Alfred A. Knopf, 1964.

Contents

Chapter	Page
Introduction	13
I. Definitions and Distinctions	23
II. Impressionist Sensibility	35
III. The Play with Reflections	51
IV. Stylistic Devices	69
Conclusion	87
Notes	115
Bibliography	143
Index	153

Illustrations

Figure 1. Eugène Delacroix: "Cheval attaqué par une Lionne," 1844   92

Figure 2. James McNeill Whistler: "Portrait of the Artist's Mother; Arrangement in Grey and Black," 1872   94

Figure 3. Camille Pissarro: "La diligence à Louveciennes," 1870   96

Figure 4. Pierre Auguste Renoir: "La Grenouillère," 1869   98

Figure 5. Claude Monet: "Régates à Argenteuil, 1872   100

Figure 6. Claude Monet: "Femme à l'Ombrelle," 1886   102

Figure 7. Claude Monet: "La Cathédrale de Rouen—plein soleil," 1894   104

Figure 8. Edgar Degas: "Aux Courses: Jockeys amateurs près d'une voiture," 1879   106

Figure 9. Vincent Van Gogh: "L'Eglise d'Auvers," 1890   108

Figure 10. Paul Cézanne: "Nature Morte aux Oignons," 1888-1900   110

Introduction

"J'achève *L'Education* avec une admiration toujours plus vive; c'est décidément une des pierres
d'angle de notre roman français."
André Gide to Roger Martin du Gard
Correspondance, Avril 25, 1925

("I've just finished the *Education Sentimentale*
with even . more admiration. It's, without a
doubt, one of the cornerstones of the French
novel.")

The purpose of this study is to provide some insights into the
importance of literary impressionism for our culture. Impressionist culture interests us, especially, by virtue of the notion
of man that it calls into consideration, and by values it trans-
mits as disclosed in the works of Flaubert, Gide, Proust, Sartre,
Robbe-Grillet or Claude Simon in France, Rilke in Germany,
and Osamu Dazai in Japan. Impressionist creations in various
countries are different expressions of the same basic idea. The
common denominator of these various literary and artistic expressions is the impressionist style. It refers to a manner of suggesting reality. It is a manner in which a given artistic effect
is achieved. Impressionism is a style which implies man's orien-
tation to a supreme value.

The physicist and philosopher, Ernst Mach, and the phenom-
enologist, Merleau-Ponty, diagnose the widespread cultural
phenomenon of impressionism. In *Die Analyse der Empfindung-
en* (1885), Mach calls spaces and times as appropriately sensations as colors and sounds. The unity of space and color sensation is for Mach and the impressionists an interplay of the individual's consciousness and the surrounding world. The reader is
intended to seize the impressionist works spatially in a moment
of time, rather than as a time sequence. The impressionist writ-

ers share with recent investigators in phenomenology the conviction that we cannot know reality independently of consciousness, and that we cannot know consciousness independently of
reality. Impressionists do not return to the thing-in-itself (Kant's
noumenon). They return to the thing which is the direct object
of consciousness, to what Kant would have called appearance of
reality in consciousness or *phenomenon*. The works of Merleau-
Ponty, and in particular his *Sens et Non-Sens* (1948) and *L'Oeil
et l'Esprit* (1964), are keys to the understanding of both the failure and the triumph of impressionism and post-impressionism
in painting.

Impressionism is born from the fundamental insight that our
consciousness is sensitive and passive. Man's consciousness faces
this world as pure passivity, a mirror in which the world inscribes
or reflects itself. As a detached spectator, the individual considers the world without having a standpoint in it. Reality is a synthesis of sense-impressions. Impressionist art suggests an emotional reality. Impressionism means a new attitude toward life.
Can we forget to "know" that the sky is blue, the grass, green;
and to say, feel, paint, or express what the eye actually "sees"?
What we actually see is a vibration of light on matter in dissolution, as Laforgue, the foremost impressionist critic explains:
"Il [un oeil naturel] arrive à voir la réalité dans l'atmosphère
vivante des formes, décomposée, réfractée, réfléchie par les êtres
et les choses, en incessantes vibrations. Telle est cette première
caractéristique de l'impressionnisme."[1] This means that, for the
impressionists, there is no idealistic mental nature: the sense-
impressions we have are nature itself. They are not appearances
of some underlying realities we can neither see, smell, nor touch,
as the symbolists would have it: on the contrary, sense impressions are experiences of the qualities of things.

Impressionist works reveal what is lyrical in art and life.
Among all the arts, it is music which naturally lends itself to
transmutation and to the creation of moods. Michel Butor, in
Les Oeuvres d'Art Imaginaires chez Proust, when examining the
descriptions of Vinteuil's sonata, in *Un Amour de Swann*, arrives

at a fundamental insight of impressionist art: Music accedes to representation by its spatiality, by the establishment of sonic space which permits the advent of articulated speech. Thus, music suggests the non-verbal thought process. Melody, harmony, rhythm, and color are the structure of impressionist creations in which emotions and moods are translated from one medium into the other. Debussy could write "Reflets dans l'Eau" for the piano, while Monet painted such reflections on canvas. A line from Baudelaire's "Harmonie du Soir" could suggest a mood for Debussy's "Les Sons et les parfums tournent dans l'air du soir." (Baudelaire said in the poem "Correspondances," "Les parfums, les couleurs, et les sons se répondent.") Rimbaud, Whistler, Debussy, Baudelaire, and Verlaine used musical titles such as "Nocturnes," "Romances sans paroles," "Effets de nuit," etc.

With the creations of Flaubert, Rilke, Gide and Proust, with Verlaine's *Art Poétique,* Baudelaire's and Rimbaud's prose poems, Paris becomes indisputably the cradle of French impressionism, literary and musical, as well as artistic. We conceive of the lyrical novel as an outgrowth of both the aesthetics of Flaubert's prose and Baudelaire's prose poems.

Flaubert has been declared the founder of literary impressionism,[2] for he presents the impressions of his protagonists without "intruding" into their world. His impassivity and impersonality reach their greatest density in *L'Education Sentimentale* of 1869. The events are seen from different centers of consciousness: the protagonists assume the function of "reflectors" or "mirrors." They see those details which are most striking from their angle of vision. It shifts, however, according to the density of light which influences their sight. The author "identifies" with the illusions of the protagonists, and ironically, the distinction between author and protagonist, between illusion and reality disappears.

In this work, Frédéric is the first example of the modern anti-hero. He is unable to understand himself. His understanding of himself seems to roll over him and then out of his grasp, like a wave across the sand. He seems unaware of his own self-deceptions. The quality of the images of light, of steam, of heat, of sound, of movement, of fog, of mist, and of the river is evocatory and atmospheric: it isolates the observer and creates the impression of vagueness and distance. These images reflect states of emotion within the main character whose vision is impaired: their quality is a psychological as well as a narrative ambience and erodes any clear distinction between reality and hallucination, between truth and illusion. There seems to be no clear continuum of events: structure and themes seem to be discontinuous because of the frequent shifts of point of view. Proust and Gide were the first to acknowledge the aesthetic revolution of Flaubert's *L'Education Sentimentale* in which "impression" replaces "action." Detachment from the human character is a stylistic device: when Flaubert dispenses with character, naturally, he has to do away with plot too. The reader sees Frédéric in successive instant portraits of fragmentary and progressive images of *anéantissement, abandon, oubli, dénuement, dépouillement, désagrégation, épuisement, dépersonnalisation,* and *dissolution.* The major impression of the book is the one of distance, of detachment, of discontinuity.

Flaubert's style reflects an impression that lingers for but a moment. Characteristics of this style[3] are devices which Flaubert shares with his impressionist successors: the strong verbs are often replaced by weak auxiliaries (*être, avoir*), by colorless verbs of perception (*paraître, sembler, glisser, osciller*), by substantivized color adjectives, by quality nouns, by impersonal synthetic pronouns, by a predominance of color over objects, by subjective impressions and by onomatopoeic overtones. There is a frequent use of ellipsis to express an absence, there are adverbial expressions to suggest a certain *Stimmung,* "mood," or "atmosphere." Flaubert initiates the use of present participles to suggest an illusion and indicate simultaneity. His composition by *tableaux* is most effective when he creates distance in the way French writers of the seventeenth century would create it: with the indefinite article, adverbs and prepositions (*avec, au-loin, par-derrière*). There are inversions, crescendo effects, a lack of outline, and a predominant shifting use of the present and imperfect. These aesthetic devices have contributed to the aesthetics of impressionist creations up to the recent works of Claude Simon, Perec, Robbe-Grillet in various forms and expressions.

Gide transformed the narrative of *La Nouvelle Education Sentimentale,* a short fragment and the original draft of *Les Cahiers d'André Walter* (1891), into the form of a diary, the form most used by impressionist writers. Writers of notebooks, diaries, and memoirs have the advantage of changing writing styles, points of view, and reveal the development of awareness of the protagonist. Gide presents two diaries, "Le Cahier Blanc" which deals with "l'amour—souvenir" and "Le Cahier Noir" in which Walter sets out to write his novel, draws up a plan for *Allain,* and formulates its aesthetic theories. This is an example of what Gide calls a *"mise en abyme,"* a retroaction of the subject on itself: it means that the pattern of the whole is reflected or mirrored in certain of its parts, it serves as a mirror of the major theme, of the narrator's self, and of the whole work. Also, when Gide wrote *Les Cahiers d'André Walter,* he felt many affinities with Flaubert's Frédéric Moreau, and still more, was deeply impressed by Flaubert's stylistic devices. The major purpose of his lyrical prose, Gide tells us, is to write not in French but in music.[4] Phenomenologically, music is anterior to spoken language, and it is in the musical structure of Gide's lyrical work that language can appear. Language is no longer understood as thought and concept, but as sensation and sound image. In this respect, Gide's *Les Nourritures Terrestres* (1897) appears to us as almost the gospel of impressionist lyrical prose. It is a hymn of joy, of spontaneity, of instantaneousness, of discontinuity, of detachment, of dissolution. All beings are judged according to their ability to receive light. The reflection of light on cities and landscapes creates the impression of distance, remoteness, and detachment. Reality for Gide's protagonist is a synthesis of pure sensations, modulated by consciousness and changed into impressions.

It is Marcel Proust who, in *Les Plaisirs et les Jours* (1896) and in his *Le Temps Retrouvé* (1927), defines reality as it presents itself to his senses in various lights and from various points of view. It is a reality free from reasoning and will. With Proust, and later Claude Simon, the act of perceiving and the act of remembering are homologous.

It seems impossible to limit impressionist and post-impressionist tendencies in lyrical prose to France. While working as Rodin's secretary in Paris (1905-06), Rilke studied the works of Flaubert, Baudelaire, Gide, and Cézanne. *Die Aufzeichnungen des Malte Laurids Brigge* was conceived in Paris and finished there. Gide was a great admirer of Rilke, as revealed by his correspondence[5] with Rilke and his translation of Rilke's work, "Les Cahiers de Malte Lauride Brigge."[6] Rilke who was less interested in Gide than in the works of both Rodin and Cézanne, translated Gide's *Le Retour de l'Enfant Prodigue* in 1913. This book has some bearing on the conclusion of Rilke's *Die Aufzeichnungen des Malte Laurids Brigge* (1906). It seems unlikely that *Les Nourritures Terrestres* which Rilke declined to translate in 1921 could have made any profound impression on Rilke in later years.[7]

In a letter to Clara (September 8, 1908), Rilke admits that Malte reflects his own poetic development, an experience which parallels the one of Cézanne: ". . . for Cézanne is nothing else but the first primitive and bare achievement of that which in M. L. was not yet achieved. Brigge's death: that was Cézanne's life, the life of his last thirty years."[8] Rodin, Cézanne, Baudelaire, and Flaubert directed his artistic observation toward objective expression, to become a sculptor in words. Malte fails to penetrate into the confidence of things, as did Flaubert's Saint-Julien-l'hospitalier; he also fails, most of his life, to realize himself in his quest for love that embraces everything, even the leper: each thing is merely a space [*Raum*], a possibility, Rilke explains in the Cézanne letter series of October 1907:

> You surely remember . . . from the *Notebooks of Malte Laurids* the passage that has to do with Baudelaire and with his poem: "The Carcass." I could not help thinking that without this poem the whole development toward objective expression, which we now think we recognize in Cézanne,

could not have started; it had to be there first in its inexorability. Artistic observation had first to have prevailed upon itself far enough to see even in the horrible and apparently merely repulsive that which is and which, with everything else that is, *is valid*. The creator is no more allowed to discriminate than he is to turn away from anything that exists: a single denial at any time will force him out of the state of grace, make him utterly sinful. Flaubert, retelling with so much discretion and care the legend of Saint-Julien-l'hospitalier, gave it that simple credibility in the midst of the miraculous, because the artist in him made the saint's resolves along with him and happily assented to them and applauded them. This lying down beside the leper and sharing with him all his own warmth, even to the heart-warmth of nights of love: this must sometime have been in the existence of an artist, as something overcome toward his new blessedness. You can imagine how it moves me to read that Cézanne in his last years still knew this very poem—Baudelaire's "Charogne"—entirely by heart and recited it word for word. . . .

And all at once (and for the first time) I understand the destiny of Malte Laurids. Isn't it this, that this test surpassed him, that he did not stand it in the actual, though of the idea of its necessity he was convinced, so much so that he sought it out instinctively until it attached itself to him and did not leave him any more? The book of Malte Laurids, when it is written sometime, will be nothing but the book of this insight, demonstrated in one for whom it was too tremendous. Yet perhaps he *did* stand it: for he wrote the death of the Chamberlain; but like Raskolnikov he was left behind, exhausted by his deed, not continuing to act at the moment when action ought just to have begun, so that his newly won freedom turned upon him and rent him, defenseless as he was.[9]

The theme of the self is of basic interest in the works of the discussed authors. They present an anti-hero who is uncertain not only of his identification in his world, but also of his identity as a self. Osamu Dazai, well acquainted with the impressionist works as seen and read both in Japan and Paris, created with

Yozo's diaries, in *No Longer Human* (1958), an impressionist
protagonist who is doomed to self-alienation: he establishes a
public concept of himself as a clown and he is not able to escape
it as long as he is part of society. These buffers which usually
protect man from Nothingness and Nausea—family, profession,
friends, relations, which are for Sartre's protagonists the social
framework, provided they are "cheating"—cannot save Yozo
from self-alienation.

The *rayonnement* of impressionist tendencies also reaches the
regions of the contemporary novel in France. A study on impressionist tendencies in lyrical prose would be incomplete, if we
would omit J.-P. Sartre in this discussion. His position might
seem out of place here: he rejects Flaubert's prose for his disen-
gagement in political and social matters (an attitude which Flaubert shares with other impressionists); Sartre considers each of
the arts on its own terms; draws a sharp distinction between
prose and poetry; between the real and the imaginary; between
existence and being.[10] Theoretically, there seems to be no
reason for including Sartre in our discussion. His *La Nausée*
(1938) and *Les Chemins de la Liberté* (1949) reflect, however,
some essential impressionist stylistic devices: form and structure
of the diary, the concept of the protagonist approaches the impressionists' attitudes toward reality. Sartre's deep interest in
phenomenology is a well-known fact. The most complete study
of Sartre's aesthetics is that of Eugene F. Kaelin, who compares
and contrasts Sartre with Merleau-Ponty, and studies the structure of the diary as used by Sartre, in *La Nausée*: "Since the
change in the diarist's attitude is from the objectivity of events
to the impression of objects upon his own inner state, the style
develops into complete *impressionism*. The people, the town, the
events are, in this style, depicted as they touch the author's consciousness, and reflect a first level of heightening subjectivity.
In this mood, given in the impressionistic style, the author is concerned primarily with the phenomenal attributes of things and
people. . . ."[11] The only other literary critic who speaks of impressionist tendencies, in Sartre's prose, is R.-M. Albérès.[12] He
also reveals the impressionist devices used by Robbe-Grillet,

Claude Simon and Nathalie Sarraute, whose work will shortly be discussed as the ultimate expression of impressionist stylistic devices.

We do not wish to analyze each work on its own, only insofar as it contributes to the evolution of literary impressionist tendencies in lyrical prose. Sometimes, cross references to impressionist creations in both music and painting might help us better to interpret the writer's stylistic devices. Two things seem to be most striking in impressionist creations: On the one hand, there is the impressionist painter, composer and writer who, in wishing to recover man's wholeness, attaches his own intuitive being to the created being, and who, paradoxically, proceeds in fragmentary impressions, reflections, and illusions of the moment. On the other hand, these impressions of a world in dissolution add up to an autonomous work of art. Detached from traditional values, all artistic impressionist creations become autonomous entities, reflecting a detachment of social, political, religious, and sacred events. Impressionist writers have lost contact with the historical and mythological worlds of classical antiquity as well as with the religious world of Scripture. Impressionism transformed the revolutionary political elements of naturalism into "an individualistic, non-transcendental world view."[13] A poem or a novel which should "not mean but be," returns to itself, not referring to anything beyond it, seeing nothing that is not within itself. The writer is neither a sensualist nor a thinker; he is primarily a maker. And to paraphrase the poet, an impressionist piece of prose doesn't mean; it is. Gide expresses this autonomy of the artist and his work: "L'état c'est moi, l'artiste! civile ou pas, mon oeuvre ne prétend concurrencer rien."[14] From this point of view, literary impressionism approaches the Flaubertian ideal of the *livre sur rien,* the "book about nothing," the self-contained work that is its own form and substance. Robbe-Grillet, in *Pour le Nouveau Roman,* confirms as much: "Nous ne croyons plus aux significations figées, toutes faites, que livrait à l'homme l'ancien ordre divin, et à sa suite l'ordre rationaliste du XIXe siècle, mais nous reportons sur l'homme tout notre espoir: ce sont les formes qu'il crée qui peuvent apporter des significations du monde."[15]

CHAPTER ONE

Definitions and Distinctions

"Le plus notable fait esthétique de cette
heure consiste en l'effort manifeste d'une
synthèse de tous les arts en chacun des
arts."

Charles Morice to Anatole France,
Demain, 1888.

("The most aesthetic feat of this time is the
manifest effort to synthesize all the arts in
each one of the arts.")

1. *The Use of the Term "Impressionism"*

To demonstrate the need for redefining the concept of impressionism in artistic creation, a few examples will illustrate how variously and how vaguely the term is used by both writers and critics. Its interpretations are at all times contradictory and mean within a given period entirely different things. Therefore, we propose to group these criticisms according to their common outlook from the midst of the 19th century up to the present moment. We hope to demonstrate their vagueness and contradictory nature within a given period, and also to illustrate the phases of the development of the notion of "impressionism."

Indeed, there is no general formula for impressionism that is valid for all artists and for all times. Although Walter Pater, in England, used the term "impressionism," in *The Renaissance* (1873), to discuss the function of the aesthetic critic, the term "impressionism" is commonly said to have been derived from Claude Monet's painting, "Impression: Soleil Levant" (1874). One of the earliest, even though vague, definitions of impressionist painting may be applied to literature by its reference to "impressionism" as a slighting of all formal values, as a non-intellectual vision, and as a confusion of the organs of sense-perception: "L'horreur de la composition est le signe caractéristique de l'impressionnisme. Il repousse tout effet obtenu par des apprêts intellectuels et subjectifs, il n'admet que les arrangements libres de la nature" (Bergerat, Journal officiel, 17 avril 1877).[1] Borrowing the term from painting, Brunetière, in 1883, is the first to apply it to literature: "Nous pourrons définir déjà l'impressionnisme littéraire une transposition systématique des moyens d'expression d'un art, qui est l'art d'écrire."[2]

As soon as the term fell into the hands of the literary critics, it was distorted, defining impressionism as a literary movement in terms of the evolution or the antithesis of an existing movement. It is an acknowledged literary movement in Danish, German and British literature,[3] whereas in French and American literature, impressionism is one of those elusive terms which writers and critics use as vaguely and variously as they use imagism, symbolism, stream of consciousness, decadent literature. Thus, even Helmut Hatzfeld's view, as expounded in his book, Literature through Art (1960), a book sharply criticized in some reviews, seems rather vague when he assumes that "from a philosophical point of view any form of modern realism can be called impressionism."[4]

Often associated with naturalism, impressionism becomes to the famous German critic Hermann Bahr "subjective naturalism," the very last achievement of classicism and a reduction of man's vision to passive sense perceptions: "Der Impressionismus ist ja nur das letzte Wort der klassischen Kunst, er vollendet und erfüllt sie ganz, indem er das äussere Sehen auf das höchste zu steigern, das innere Sehen soviel als möglich auszuschalten, 'das Eigenleben,' die Selbsttätigkeit, den Willen des Auges immer mehr abzuschwächen sucht und so den Menschen zum völligen Passivium seiner Sinne macht."[5] For Zola, in Salon de 1880, the terms "impressionism," "naturalism," and "modernism" have no distinctive meaning. Realizing the importance of light effects in both painting and literature, he stresses the influence of impressionist (or realist) painting on Stendhal, Balzac, and Flaubert.

Other studies, determining the nature of impressionism as the evolution of or reaction against an existing movement, seem to be generalizations which are the reason for so many contradictions. Impressionism includes both realism and naturalism in reaction against symbolism for Georg Loesch.[6] He calls Balzac, Flaubert, and Zola "impressionists" in his 1919 study of the style of the Goncourts who, since Desprez' book on *L'évolution naturaliste* in 1884, have been called the major representatives of impressionism. At the end of the nineteenth century impressionism is called a natural evolution of romanticism,[7] whereas in the 1950's impressionism seems to be the logical development of naturalism,[8] and at the same time it is labeled a reaction against the objectivity of realism and a revolt against human passions, and as such against romanticism.[9] The common view of these critics, so contradictory they appear to be, is to establish the essence of impressionism in the late nineteenth century, and recognize it as a historical phenomenon. Venturi summarizes their common attempt: "The essence of Impressionism can be found only in the historical phenomenon of Impressionism."[10]

The term "literary impressionism"[11] is not only vaguely defined in connection with other literary movements, but also when defined by synonyms.[12] Its association with phenomenology, however, is most justifiable when used by critics, such as Gustave Geffroy in 1894, Bally in 1936, and Albérès in 1966 and 1970. Gustave Geffroy, in *Vie Artistique*,[13] defines an impressionist painting as a kind of painting that approaches phenomenology, tending to represent the appearance and meaning of objects in space, and attempting to synthesize these things in the semblance of a moment. Bally, in *Mélanges d'histoire littéraire et de philologie* offerts à M. Bernard Bouvier, Geneva 1920, distinguishes an "impressionist" or "phenomenological" and a "causal" or "transitive" form of perception.[14] With the impressionists' perceptive experience, the reality of the novel changes; the

traditional frozen forms of description (Balzac) set themselves
into motion spatially. The protagonists see reality from several
angles of vision at once and the objects are released without losing sight of their earlier positions.[15] Referring to this new reality
of the novel, the critic R.-M. Albérès when discussing the *roman
artistique,* the "artistic novel" and *roman phénoménologique,*
the "phenomenological novel," in *Métamorphoses du roman,* sees
an analogy between phenomenology and impressionism in the
contemporary works of Musil and Proust:

> Avec eux et avec leurs contemporains apparaît une inten-
> tion que l'on pourra appeler "phénoménologique" et que
> confirma la vogue de la phénoménologie chez les phi-
> losophes et les critiques après 1940. Dans cet univers in-
> décis où se mêlent subjectivisme et objectivité, le roman n'est
> plus une histoire, mais une mêlée de sensations, d'impres-
> sions, d'expériences. Il n'est pas "tout fait," présenté à
> l'avance, mis en forme et sous emballage par un conteur
> expérimenté. Il est proposé au lecteur comme une matière
> fluide, poétique, énigmatique, et au lieu d'y suivre le fil
> d'une intrigue, on y errera comme dans un rêve, ou comme
> dans la vie. . . . chez Proust, chez Musil, chez Kafka, peut-
> être chez Joyce et chez Virginia Woolf (puis chez Michel
> Butor et Alain Robbe-Grillet), tout se trouve inversé: *ce
> n'est plus le héros du roman qui est situé dans le monde où
> il vit; mais c'est la vision du monde "réel" qui est soumise aux
> rapports du héros et du monde* . . . c'est la conscience du
> héros du roman qui domine le roman, et le "monde réel"
> n'existera que dans la mesure où il est reflété par cette
> conscience.
>   A cette vision romanesque, on aurait donné en 1890 la
> qualification d' "impressionniste" ou de "subjectiviste." On
> dit de nos jours "phénoménologique."[16]

With the impressionists' erosion of contours, the fragmentation
of form and matter, a similar trend can be observed in science.
Therefore, the views of the art critic René Huyghe and Professor
Henri Simon[17] seem most valid since they call attention to a

parallel movement in science, a movement which is identical with intellectual relativism and which introduces an atomized vision of the world. Also, scientific thought had a strong impact on impressionist art. Chevreul's *Law of Simultaneous Contrasts and Colors* (1838) and Helmholtz' studies on the physiology and psychology of color vision (about 1880) undoubtedly affected the impressionists:

> Science et impressionnisme, chacun en son domaine, pourraient se résumer par la même formule, le même programme: un sensualisme rationnel. . . . Impressionnisme - vision de l'univers nouveau . . . La Science divise la matière en milliards d'atomes qui font de l'univers un immense magma de particules infinitésimales qui tourbillonnent et où les hasards et la logique des associations créent les corps, les formes, les objets, comme autant de provisoires phantasmes? L'impressionniste de son côté pratique un semblable divisionnisme: plus de contours, plus de formes, plus d'objets distincts; un poudroiement de taches colorées dont le rapprochement, le groupement engendrent l'illusion des choses. La même poésie profonde, la même vision lyrique s'y manifestent.[18]

The impressionists' lyrical approach to reality often misled critics to assimilate their attempts with those of the symbolists. Rimbaud, in "Délires II," speaks of having invented the colors of vowels and a poetic language accessible to all the senses. The symbolists about 1888, indeed, took his sonnet, "Voyelles," as an offspring of the Baudelairian doctrine of *correspondances* whereby a word is seen as capable of provoking sensory responses. Ruth Moser, in her monumental book on French impressionism,[19] does not draw any sharp distinction between symbolism and impressionism; yet it has become an acknowledged fact that there are two different aesthetics at the basis of impressionism and symbolism.[20] Impressionism, as Michel Décaudin tells us, "s'attache au réel, fixe l'éphémère; l'autre est tourné vers l'absolu, le rêve et l'idéal."[21] The symbolist, spiritualistic and idealistic in outlook, seeks an escape from reality in an ideal "Absolute," while the impressionist, having no faith at all in transcendental values, lives "earth to earth" both enjoying and passively undergoing instantaneous impressions. With the impressionists, life becomes (as Virginia Woolf would have it) "a luminous halo" whose "myriad impressions" they wish to render the "semitransparent envelope."

Despite all the vagueness of what may be called an impressionist tendency in literature, it is a critical commonplace that all impressionists are to a certain extent expressionists.[22] The concept of character and stylistic devices, and the form and structure of the novel reflect this change from impressionism to expressionism in all works prior to the *nouveau roman*. Often, in literature, impressionist passivity becomes expressionist activity, and both objects and subjects start to move as they are seen with their symbolic and emotive character, in a conscious distortion and abstraction.[23] This change from impressionism to expressionism occurs also within the protagonists; it is a change from impressionist to expressionist attitudes. There is, on the one hand, the passive impressionist protagonist who usually ends in a state of dissolution or in self-destruction (Flaubert's Frédéric Moreau and Emma Bovary, Gide's Narcissus, Joyce's Stephen Dedalus, Sartre's Roquentin, Rilke's Malte Laurids, Osamu Dazai's Yozo). If that same protagonist, however, not only sought the mirror of his self in things, but used these things to convey messages from his inner world, and at the same time, felt free to deform natural appearance to express feelings in accord with his inner necessity, then he no longer perceived the world as phenomenon. As an emotional reaction to the outside world, such art became a symbol of the protagonist's emotions and of his expressionist attitude toward the world. This change from an impressionist to an expressionist attitude toward the world, we can observe in Malte Laurids. First, like Baudelaire, he accepts the great city as real without wishing to escape the reality of its disease and putridity. When Malte tries to rise out of a muddy, unreflective, impressionistic state and attempts to return to an awareness of himself, he finds himself at the brink of an abyss (which he identifies with the street), hollow spaces opening up before him. He tries to escape, yet feels immobile. All our comprehension of Malte's situation is delivered in terms of a basic emotion, fear. The flickering, unstable, semi-transparent moment-to-moment being of consciousness, the shifting way in which it conceives objects and itself, uses a broken language, mirror of the innermost part of the soul. Thus, the ways of seeing the city reflect Malte's impressionist and expressionist attitudes in both language and imagery.

This change from impressionism to expressionism occurs not only within a given work of art, but even within a given passage. Van Gogh, starting to paint an impressionist portrait of one of his artist friends, suddenly feels the inner necessity to express his emotions in colors independent from the object under consideration.[24] In literature, the same phenomenon occurs within a paragraph as early as with Flaubert; he uses verbs instead of the impressionistic nouns and adjectives to express both the motion and emotion of both the subjects and objects. Later, the Goncourts' *Manette Salomon*, as Ullman points out, is "a novel in which even inanimate objects can be brought to life and endowed with human characteristics. The objects are seen as the real protagonists, they are in the forefront, and the human element is only incidentally mentioned and merely provides the background of the scene."[25] Rimbaud's "Fleurs,"[26] Joyce's *A Portrait of the Artist*, Rilke's *Notebook of Malte Laurids Brigge,* and Dazai Osamu's *No Longer Human* are the finest illustrations of this change from impressionism to expressionism. Thus, we may agree with Hatzfeld that both impressionist stylistic devices and human attitudes slowly developed into expressionistic-surrealistic forms.[27]

2. *The Historical Phenomenon of Impressionism*

In this essay we wish to establish the notion in Western Europe[28] of "impressionist literature" within a given period. Many critics[29] conceive of impressionism as a permanent ten-

dency of all the arts, a *Stil der Erschöpfung*,[30] "decadent style"
or an "illusionism"[31] throughout the centuries, from the middle
ages to the twentieth century with a climax in the late nineteenth
century, when the interpenetration of the arts is bound up with
the interpenetration of sensations; when color and sounds follow
the same principles as words, then Baudelaire's dream seems to
be realized: there is a unity in art appealing to all the senses together. With the impressionists, painting becomes a form of art
which is closely related to music and poetry, and likewise, literature to painting and music, and music to painting and literature.
This new relationship between poetry and painting, and letters
and art is all-important.

There is some agreement among critics that literary impressionism can be limited to a particular period of taste. The way
impressionist writers saw the physical world and apprehended
reality was shaped by pictorial experience: the impressionist generation of painters was born between 1830 and 1841 (Pissarro in
1830, Manet in 1832, Degas in 1834, Cézanne and Sisley in 1839,
Monet in 1840, Renoir, Bazille and Morisot in 1841). The masters
of impressionist painting were active as late as the fourth dec-
ade of our century: Degas and Rodin died in 1917, Renoir in
1919, Monet in 1926, Signac in 1935, the year of Liebermann's
death, Germany's greatest impressionist painter. Flaubert and
the Goncourts, Conrad and Lawrence have extended into literature the method of the French impressionist painters. The deep
influence of Rodin and Cézanne on Rilke, of Vermeer and the
impressionist artists on Proust, is a critical commonplace. For
Henry James too, the analogy between the art of the painter and
the art of the novelist is complete. Michel Décaudin[32] establishes
the presence of *un courant impressionniste,* an "impressionist
tendency," in poetry and rather obscure prose between 1867 and
1885, a parallel to the movement in painting. Hamann declares
it "the dominating style of all the arts between 1874 and 1914,"[33]
and Hatzfeld locates it between 1860 and 1910.[34] But impressionism actually was anticipated by Balzac in 1832.

However, not all literary impressionism can be explained by

the influence of painting. Both Flaubert[35] and the Goncourts[36] use impressionist stylistic techniques before they have been acquainted with the major works of impressionist painters.

In literature, aesthetic theory and criticism precede the realization of impressionist style. Novelists first present painters who expound theories closely related to impressionist aesthetics.[37] Balzac, in *Le Chef-d'Oeuvre Inconnu* (February, 1832), presents a painter, Frenhofer, who calls into question the plasticity of solids, their form and design, the surrounding atmosphere, and the suggestive colors of a fragment. The incredible foresight of Balzac, says Rilke in a letter to Clara, is that there are actually "no contours at all, only countless vibrating planes merging into one another."[38] For this reason, Cézanne identified himself with Frenhofer, and said repeatedly: "Frenhofer, c'est moi."[39] The Goncourts, too, discuss impressionist painters in *Manette Salomon* (1864-66), recommending Trouville as an ideal spot for painters. Zola's *L'Oeuvre* (1886) is a novel about the failure of impressionism as presented by Zola's fictional transformation of Cézanne into Claude Lantier, the *artiste manqué*, the "artistic failure." Despite its failure, Zola in his "Le Naturalisme au Salon" conceives of impressionism as an influential tendency of modern art:

> Le grand malheur, c'est que pas un artiste de ce groupe n'a réalisé puissamment et définitivement la formule qu'ils apportent tous éparse dans leurs oeuvres. La formule est là, divisée à l'infini; mais nulle part, dans aucun d'eux, on ne la trouve appliquée par un maître. Ce sont tous des précurseurs, l'homme de génie n'est pas né. . . . ils restent inférieurs à l'oeuvre qu'ils tentent, ils bégayent sans pouvoir trouver le mot. . . . Mais leur influence n'en reste pas moins énorme, car ils sont dans la seule évolution possible, ils marchent à l'avenir.[40]

There is enough evidence, however, that soon after 1880 impressionism became an international movement, literary and musical as well as artistic. Paris is indisputably the cradle of French impressionism with Verlaine's *Art Poétique, Croquis Parisiens, Romances sans Paroles* (1366-84), Proust's *Les Plaisirs et les Jours,* (1896), Laforgue's *Mélanges Posthumes* (1903), Gide's *Les Cahiers et les Poésies d'André Walter* (1891), and *Les Nour-ritures Terrestres* (1897). Paris attracted many writers whose early work is impressionistic: Oscar Wilde and George Moore from England; James Joyce from Ireland; Stefan George, Rilke, Hofmannsthal and Liliencron from Germany and Austria; Azorin and Miró from Spain; D'Annunzio from Italy; Rodenbach and Verhaeren from Belgium; Chekhov from Russia; and Dazai Osamu from Japan. Impressionism became a Parisian movement with cosmopolitan character. No matter how closely bound up with French culture, impressionism ranges further than that culture, transcends it, and thus cannot be linked to any national group, even though one cannot conceive of impressionism without Paris.

Precursors of British and American impressionism (E. A. Poe, Swinburne, Walt Whitman, Oscar Wilde, and Conrad) were widely read by Chekhov, Baudelaire, Rimbaud, Mallarmé, Debussy, and D'Annunzio. Their aesthetic principles became the basis of impressionist style in literature. Well accepted and assimilated in France, these principles were again formally introduced to both English and American literature. George Moore's first novel, *A Modern Lover* (1883),[41] has been claimed to be most influential in this respect. Impressionist aesthetics had its impact in turn on Virginia Woolf, Ford Madox Hueffer, D. H. Lawrence, Katherine Mansfield, E. M. Forster, Henry James, Dos Passos, Stephen Crane, Gertrude Stein, and William Faulkner in prose; Wallace Stevens, John Gould Fletcher, and Amy Lowell in poetry.[42]

Another important mutation of British and American impressionism took place with the first editions of the work of Henry James and Joseph Conrad in France, as R.-M. Albérès points out: "Dès l'apparition de Henry James et de Joseph Conrad, l'art de

Nathalie Sarraute, de Michel Butor, et même d'Alain Robbe-Grillet est né."[43]

With Albérès[44] and Francastel,[45] we conclude that impressionism is not limited to a short period, its high point in 1875 and its end in 1885. Even though the painter Paul Signac (1863-1935), in *D'Eugène Delacroix au Néo-Impressionnisme,* implies that impressionism ceased to exist at a certain date, it remains the predominant style to the present day in literature. Alhough painting dominated all the other arts in the years 1875-85, impressionism in literature developed its own style and techniques. Impressionist creations in various countries are different expressions of the same basic idea, and may be recognized as being merely different symptoms in the same general syndrome. Impressionism is still alive today as Francastel asserts: "Il est ainsi évident que les circonstances et les causes de l'évolution survenue vers 1885 ne peuvent aboutir à déterminer la manière dont l'impressionnisme a cédé le pas à d'autres mouvements de même conséquence pour l'histoire de l'art et de la culture. Impossible, par suite, de définir le moment, les circonstances et les causes du déclin d'un mouvement qui est devenu une forme-type de l'esprit."[46] In this sense, impressionism has become the core of our "instant culture." The impressionist painters' views of the problems which confront modern writers are as true and relevant today as when they expressed them in the years 1875-85. A climate of impressionism that crosses the mediums of literature, painting, sculpture, music, criticism, philosophy, and science existed and still exists.

CHAPTER TWO

Impressionist Sensibility

"Zum sehen geboren, zum schauen bestellt"
Goethe, *Faust II.*

("To see I was born, to look is my call")

1. The Appearance of Reality in Consciousness

While traditional writers and painters started from a definable subject, that is, experience previously organized and interpreted by the observing mind, impressionist artists started from perception. They rejected the traditional emphasis upon order, thought, and clearness. Through sensory experience, the impressionist opens a new relationship with the everyday world. Its stimulus affects the senses; the senses affect the mind. The tradition of intellectualism, which reaches back to Descartes, is enriched by an understanding of perceptual consciousness. The Cartesian defense of knowledge, "I think, therefore I am," is widened by the defense of sensation as André Gide puts it in *Les Nourritures Terrestres*: "I see, I feel, I hear, I smell; therefore I am." This sensory experience is a synthetic, intuitive feeling of oneness with reality. With impressionism, the gap between sensual experience and thought seems to be widened. Can, however, the distance between sensual experience and thought be reduced to the difference between impressions and ideas? Sensory experience and thinking are two different modes of being in the world; one does not exclude the other, as we learn from Proust. Impressionist writers did not try to reach a physical and moral ideal beyond sensation, but only within the limits of their own sensations. The novel is a subjective experience and communi-

35

cates not ideas but subjective impressions: "Seule l'impression,
si chétive qu'en semble la matière, si insaisissable la trace, est
un critérium de vérité, et à cause de cela mérite seule d'être
appréhendée par l'esprit. . . ."[1] La réalité à exprimer résidait, je
le comprenais maintenant, non dans l'apparence du sujet, mais à
une profondeur où cette apparence importait peu, comme le
symbolisaient ce bruit de cuiller sur une assiette, cette raideur
empesée de la serviette, qui m'avaient été plus précieux pour
mon renouvellement spirituel que tant de conversations humani-
taires, patriotiques, internationalistes et métaphysiques."[2] The
perceived world for the impressionists is neither a sum of objects,
the solid reality of matter, the brute reality of an inhuman world
divorced from the subject, in the tradition of realists and natural-
ists, nor is it a symbol of a hidden reality, a representation of
both idea and the unseen, the embodiment and revelation of the
infinite, in the tradition of symbolist writers.

Reality is a subject which cannot be analyzed, according to
the impressionists, but only seized intuitively. Reality is a synthesis of pure sensations, modulated by consciousness and
changed into impressions. Marcel Proust gives us the finest definition of the impressionist's concept of reality in *Le Temps Retrouvé*. Reality, for Proust, is not in the thing in itself, such as in
the grandeur of a steeple, or in the madeleine itself. Reality has
its hidden existence, revealed only by sense impressions. Reality
is a certain connection between immediate sensations: an hour is
not merely an hour, it is a vase full of scents and sounds and
projects and climates. Only the impression is a criterion for
reality, it is in the distant sound of an airplane, in the outline
of the steeple of Saint Hilaire, or in the taste of a madeleine.
Proust rejects the literature of description. If one is rational only,
one by-passes reality: "Comment la littérature de notations
aurait-elle une valeur quelconque, puisque c'est sous de petites
choses comme celles qu'elle note que la réalité est contenue (la
grandeur dans le bruit lointain d'un aéroplane, dans la ligne du
clocher de Saint-Hilaire, le passé dans la saveur d'une madeleine,
etc.) et qu'elles sont sans signification par elles-mêmes si on ne

l'en dégage pas?"[3] Also, with the impressionists, sky, earth, trees no longer have an existence in themselves; they are just the reflection of what they are traditionally considered to be. The impressionists had seen the world subjectively, as it presented itself to their senses in various lights and from various points of view. The keyboard of each impressionist artist differs; there is nothing in common between Monet's cathedrals and Cézanne's still-lifes. Emile Zola, in his *Salon de 1865*, anticipated impressionism in saying that an artist should express his personality and his temperament, and not reproduce reality. This means that the impressionist writer or painter does not form impressions from solid reality but from the appearance of reality. This, of course, is the essential condition in art without which there can be no art. With the impressionists, however, the act of seeing is painted: this means that they do not render the object itself but their way of seeing an object by a sensation. This is the most striking characteristic of impressionist art, as the art critic Venturi points out in referring to the impressionists: "the grasping of appearance is a form of sensation, sensation as free from reasoning and will as it can possible be."[4] This aesthetic principle recalls Schopenhauer's statement of the artistic procedure as the contemplation of the world independently of the principle of reason.

With impressionist literature, language is no longer understood as thought and as concept, but as sensation and sound image. Impressionists state phenomena in the order of their perception, before they have been distorted into intelligibility. The grammatical shift places the emphasis on the sensory quality of the visual experience rather than on the thing itself. Joseph Conrad tells us in 1897: "the artistic aim when expressing itself in written words must also make its appeal through the senses, if its high desire is to reach the secret spring of responsive emotions. It must strenuously aspire to the plasticity of sculpture, to the color of painting, and to the magic suggestiveness of music."[5] This view is further developed by the recent findings of Merleau-Ponty in phenomenology who, speaking of Proust, defines the writer's work as a work of language rather than of thought: "In literature, ideas, as in music and painting, are not the ideal of the intellect, they are never quite detached from what the author sees. They are transparent, as unchallengeable as persons, but not definable."[6]

According to Roger Fry (1886-1934), one can distinguish two major modes of impressionism: impressionistic creations reflecting reality as "atmospheric effects, as in Monet"; and those which represent it "as an oblique angle of vision, as in Degas."[7] Pissarro called these methods of seeing reality "romantic" (Monet, Renoir) and "scientific" (Degas, Seurat, Cézanne) impressionism. The great discovery of both impressionism and phenomenology is the existence of a bridge between consciousness and the world. The tree which I perceive as a unity and totality appears as a real tree only against the horizon of the landscape of other trees and the sky where it grows. Therefore, in writing, the word *Stimmung*, "atmosphere," or *états d'âme* becomes all-important. This fusion of the individual's consciousness with the world creates a unity between visual appearance and mental reality. In his perceptive study on literary impressionism, Sommerhalder explains: "Wenn wir uns in Stimmung befinden, dass Aussen und Innen gleichgestimmt sind, dann its die Voraussetzung dafür gegeben, dass das Ich und Weltgefühl zusammenfallen, Aussen- und Innenraum in einem einzigen Raum aufgehoben sind. Die Stimmung ist . . . das Medium, in dem die Welt der impressionistischen Dichtung zur Kondensation kommt."[8] In contrast to the impressionists, Cézanne did not put the dividing line between the senses and intelligence, but between the spontaneous order of perceived objects and the human order of ideas and of science. Merleau-Ponty significantly points out: "Il ne met pas la coupure entre 'les sens' et 'l'intelligence,' mais entre l'ordre spontané des choses perçues et l'ordre humain des idées et des sciences."[9] With the post-impressionists, vision and thought are inseparable from each other: also for Proust those impressions are most valuable which life communicates to us against our will in an impression which is material: it enters us through the senses. He, then, extracts the spiritual meaning of the given sensations. The impression is for the writer what the experiment is for the scientist. Proust tells us: "L'impression est pour l'écrivain ce qu'est l'expérimentation pour le savant, avec cette différence que chez le savant le travail de l'intelligence précède et chez l'écrivain vient après."[10] Understanding impressionist sensibility, then, involves an enormous expansion of the faculties of sensual perception and a new sharpening of sensibility, because now the intellect alone is totally incapable of grasping time, motion and life. These are the values which impressionist writers such as Conrad try to grasp intuitively in a synthesis. Conrad also wishes the reader to become a "sensitive plate": "My task which I'm trying to achieve is, by the power of the written word to make you hear, to make you feel—it is, before all, to make you see. . . ."[11]

We have seen that impressionist writers begin like the painters with an empirical reality rather than with an abstract idea. Their vision is a vision felt rather than imagined. It is a vision in which everything stable and coherent is dissolved and assumes the character of the unfinished, the fragmentary. W. B. Yeats says of this vision that things fall apart. The center cannot hold. Atomization of the world of the mind and of matter as well as relativism and subjectivism characterize the impressionist synthetic vision of the world. In this vision everything turns around sensual impression: things turned into light and color effects and into barely tangible shapes, as the poet and critic Laforgue explains: "L'impressionniste voit et rend la nature telle qu'elle est, c'est-à-dire uniquement en vibrations colorées. Ni dessin, ni lumière, ni modelé, ni perspective, ni clair-obscur, ces classifications enfantines: tout cela se résout en réalité en vibrations colorées et doit être obtenu sur la toile uniquement par vibrations colorées. . . . L'objet et le sujet sont donc irrémédiablement mouvants, insaisissables et insaisissants."[12]

Life exists for the impressionists only where there are colors, sounds, the outdoors, and the sun. With Gide's Narcissus they confirm: "Je ne veux t'enseigner d'autre sagesse que la vie!"[13] In this connection the question arises, what are our sensations of color? With the impressionists, the color of an object is not something which belongs to the object but, rather, a product of the ways in which sunlight, shadow, and reflected light play upon it. In traditional literature, color is a frequently used metaphor in the ordinary sense of vividness or piquancy, but when it is an impressionist literary creation, the meaning of such words as "red," "blue," "hot," and "cold" becomes an important question, when we think, for example, of Sartre's Roquentin. Colors produce in Roquentin similar feelings to those of touch. Color is susceptible to change, and is therefore alive. This is what Roquentin has discovered: things are alive as he is. Roquentin thinks with things and not about them. Color, temperatures, etc., are sensations which have been variously defined as ways in which a consciousness is affected and also as properties of the objects themselves. Therefore, the critic Albérès defines impressionist literature as a *plongée dans la conscience,* a "plunge into the consciousness." "Multiple, tourbillonnante, faite de poussières lumineuses suspendues dans le vide, la réalité impressionniste ne se *raconte* pas, ne se *décrit* même point. Les paroles, les gestes menus des hommes, hésitations et arabesques, indiquent à peine quelques lignes, à la surface de cette nébuleuse qui est la réalité, qui est la 'Vie.' Le lecteur est ainsi transporté dans un univers en fusion, déconcerté par une optique nouvelle . . . Loin de la vision objective, l'impressionnisme en effet est une plongée dans la conscience."[14] Consciousness, for the impressionists, is a game of reflections; it is shine and countershine. Reality, then, is seen as a harmony of subjects and objects, which merge together in terms of time and space, during any act of the protagonist, that is, their states melt into one another. Their perception of reality is determined by both time and space.

The act of perception is more important than either the perceived or the perceiver. No longer is there ME (the narrator-protagonist) on the one hand, and that tree on the other hand; there is only my seeing, retaining, or remembering that tree. The objects which each work contains are the successive contents of the consciousness, that of the narrator. There is no separation between the narrator and the objects: there is a narrator seeing the objects and without objects there can be no self, and without a self there can be no objects. Claude Simon and Robbe-Grillet agree with the phenomenological outlook of Sartre that an object is not important *per se,* only in its relationship to the consciousness in which it has appeared. Consciousness must be consciousness of something. We hope to clarify this view in the following chapter dealing with the self-reflexive function of the protagonists.

With both Proust and Claude Simon, the act of perceiving and the act of remembering are homologous. Sense impression becomes an impression in the reflective consciousness, receding into the past and evoking other impressions. With them, the act of perceiving or remembering becomes all-important. Their sentence structure and their use of the present participle place the emphasis on the sensory quality of the visual experience rather than on the thing itself. Both Proust and Claude Simon stress the discontinuity of remembered experience, as our perceptions are discontinuous. Claude Simon summarizes his hopeless endeavor to bridge the gap between the act of perception and the act of reflection, and to make the act of perceiving and the act of remembering a homologous experience: "J'étais hanté par deux choses: la discontinuité, l'aspect fragmentaire des émotions que l'on éprouve et qui ne sont jamais reliées les unes aux autres et en même temps leur contiguité dans la conscience. Ma phrase cherche à traduire cette contiguité. L'emploi du participe présent me permet de me placer hors du temps conventionnel. Lorsqu'on dit: il alla à tel endroit, on donne l'impression d'une action qui a un commencement et une fin. Or, il n'y a ni commencement ni fin dans le souvenir."[15] Impressionist writers share with recent investigators in phenomenology the conviction that we cannot know reality independently of consciousness, and that we cannot know consciousness independently of reality. Proust, Joyce, Woolf, N. Sarraute and Claude Simon dwell on their characters' memories since present consciousness cannot be isolated from previous acts of consciousness. Impressionists don't return to the thing-in-itself (Kant's *noumenon*). They return to the thing which is the direct object of consciousness, to what Kant would have called appearance of reality in consciousness or *phenomenon*.

2. Harmonies of Light and Color: Pictorial Music

Both impressionists and symbolists are preoccupied with images of light. For the symbolists, following the Platonic tradition, light is the equivalent of the highest spiritual principles, existing apart from matter, opening up a world not only beyond space and matter, but also beyond measurement. With the impressionists, light loses all such sacrosant connotations. They do not assimilate light to the Good, the True, the Beautiful, God, or the universal soul, but to their own soul. Light is the soul of impressionist paintings, and the soul of impressionist literature. It is an element of style.

Whatever we perceive is not material things, but only colors and sounds: color is not in the objects, but in the light. Therefore, what we receive from the impressionists' work is light, not the objects which reflect the light. This seems to be the greatest contribution to modern art, and Zola in his *Salon de 1876* emphasizes the importance of color and light: "La découverte de ceux d'ici [Impressionnistes] consiste proprement à avoir reconnu que la grande lumière *décolore* les tons, que le soleil reflété par les objets tend, à force de clarté, à les ramener à cette unité lumineuse qui fond ses sept rayons prismatiques en un seul éclat incolore, qui est la lumière. Ils décomposent et se constituent la lumière, dans la clarté brillante du plein jour."[16] Zola tells us, in his *Salon de 1880*, that the exhaustive analysis of the properties of color and light is the essence of impressionism: "Cette étude de la lumière dans ses milles décompositions et recompositions, est ce qu'on a appelé plus ou moins proprement l'impressionnisme, parce qu'un tableau devient dès lors l'impression d'un moment éprouvé devant la nature."[17]

The quality of light in impressionist literature is a psychological as well as a narrative ambience; it envelops both protagonists and scenes. This light never dramatizes action, but lends it calm. The works of both Flaubert and Gide seem to be the most representative of the usage of these devices, although neither author has yet been discussed in this context by critics. We wish to explore their imagery of light as it calls forth a mutation of both scenes and protagonists, and creates a new concept of allusive space.

Sometimes a protagonist is light personified, illuminating or dissolving itself. Mme. Arnoux, in *L'Education Sentimentale,* is for Frédéric Moreau such an apparition, recalling many a painting by Monet, in which he presents his wife with a parasol. In an atmosphere of daydreaming, Frédéric is floating about, vaguely suspended in a mood of hopelessness and frustration, not having been able to come close enough to the "point lumineux où l'ensemble des choses convergeait."[18] At dusk Frédéric seems to fade away like the setting sun, to become a soulless ghost in a grey and closed-up city. The distance separating Frédéric from his luminous vision is created by calculated sensory effects of the city at dusk when it is growing cold, when carriages are scattering: thus Flaubert conceives of light as occupying space, indicating the distance separating Frédéric from his ideal. Flaubert shares this concept with impressionist painters who use light to play up the instability of objects and persons, to erode symmetry and order, to suggest rather than delineate. Reality, for Frédéric, is a luminous dimension. "Les rues étaient désertes. Quelquefois une charrette lourde passait, ébranlant les pavés. Les maisons se succédaient avec leurs façades grises, leurs fenêtres closes; et il songeait dédaigneusement à tous ces êtres humains couchés derrière ces murs, qui existaient sans la voir, et dont pas un même ne se doutait qu'elle vécût! Il n'avait plus conscience du milieu, de l'espace, de rien; et, battant le sol du talon, en frappant avec sa canne les volets des boutiques, il allait toujours devant lui, au hasard, éperdu, entraîné. Un air humide l'enveloppa; ils se reconnut au bord des quais."[19]

For a writer looking at urban life, a subject already marvelously rich in poetic subject matter,[20] the atmosphere of the city becomes a vibration of light and color. When Frédéric, in *L'Education Sentimentale*, perceives the wet, wide pavements of the boulevard, the artificial lights at nightfall, and the city crowd in a fluid movement of waves, the reader is inclined to associate this evocation with either Pissarro's "Boulevard des Italiens" or Monet's "Boulevard des Capucines":

Quelquefois, l'espoir d'une distraction l'attirait vers les boulevards. Après de sombres ruelles exhalant des fraîcheurs humides, il arrivait sur de grandes places désertes, éblouissantes de lumière, et où les monuments dessinaient au bord du pavé des dentelures d'ombre noire. Mais les charrettes, les boutiques recommençaient, et la foule l'étourdissait,—le dimanche surtout,—quand, depuis la Bastille jusqu'à la Madeleine, c'était un immense flot ondulant sur l'asphalte, au milieu de la poussière, dans une rumeur continue; il se sentait tout écoeuré par la bassesse des figures, la niaiserie des propos, la satisfaction imbécile transpirant sur les fronts en sueur! Cependant, la conscience de mieux valoir que ces hommes atténuait la fatigue de les regarder.[21]

In *Les Nourritures Terrestres*, the cities of Florence and Rome, which are perceived momentarily and immediately fade away, are dissolved in light. They are seen from a distance, corroded by the vibration of light, an effect of the decomposition of light. All beings are judged according to their ability to receive light: "J'appris [Ménalque speaking to Nathanaël] à juger tous les êtres à leur capacité de réception lumineuse."[22] Light penetrates everywhere when the protagonist is ready to become the *nouvel être*, the "new being."[23] Light over Rome plainly exults Gide's Narcissus; moonlight in Amalfi evokes a deserted ocean, a dead village; sunset in Malte calls forth a special *exaltation*. Even *Narcissus* is only a vision and can disappear like light: each instant, however, seen in a new light, brings a new visual awareness of Narcissus, as well as his final dissolution: "Car, as-tu remarqué que dans ce livre il n'y avait *personne*. Et même moi, je n'y suis rien que Vision. . . . J'ai gardé jusqu'à la fin de la nuit l'espoir d'une nouveauté de lumière."[24]

It is through light and color that painting, too, attempts to rise above physical limitations: Renoir's "Bather" is a harmony of red-yellow-blue relationships, much like a major chord in music. Gide's Nathanaël seeks light, and projects onto it echoes of his individual being; and thanks to this anology, he is able to make light the language of his innermost nature. Nathanaël himself, then, becomes an element of the universe, and is no longer isolated from it:

> Tu n'imagines pas, Nathanaël, ce que peut devenir enfin cet abreuvement de lumière; et la sensuelle extase que donne cette persistante chaleur . . . Une branche d'olivier dans le ciel; le ciel au-dessus des collines; un chant de flute à la porte d'un café. . . . Alger semblait si chaude et pleine de fêtes que j'ai voulu la quitter pour trois jours; mais à Blidah, où je me réfugiais, j'ai trouvé les orangers tout en fleurs . . .
>
> Je sors dès le matin; je me promène; je ne regarde rien et vois tout; une symphonie merveilleuse se forme et s'organise en moi des sensations inécoutées. L'heure passe; mon émoi s'alentit, comme la marche du soleil moins verticale se fait plus lente. Puis je choisis, être ou chose, de quoi m'éprendre, mais je le veux mouvant, car mon émotion, sitôt fixée, n'est plus vivante. Il me semble alors à chaque instant nouveau n'avoir encore rien vu, rien goûté. Je m'éperds dans une désordonnée poursuite de choses fuyantes. Je courus hier des collines qui dominent Blidah, pour voir un peu plus longtemps le soleil; pour voir se coucher le soleil et les nuages ardents colorer les terrasses blanches. Je surprends l'ombre et le silence sous les arbres; je rôde dans la clarté de la lune; j'ai la sensation souvent de nager, tant l'air lumineux et chaud m'enveloppe et mollement me soulève.[25]

A world arises in which everything seems to have lost its natural identity. The frontier of the protagonist's self is not the surface of the skin, but the outer limits of his perception. Fusion of the world with the soul of the protagonist comes to us like a chant, and thus a new universe of words and sounds arises, a world without finitude, held together only by sounds, light, and color. The reflections of light on this reality create the impression of remoteness, distance, and detachment.

While discussing Nietzsche's aesthetic viewpoint, Gide's protagonist Edouard reveals that the impression of distance and of objects receding into a remoteness which extends in every direction, is an ideal for him: "il n'a jamais connu, le roman, cette 'formidable érosion des contours,' dont parle Nietzsche."[26] Precisely such an erosion of contours through the reflection of light is characteristic of impressionist painting, music, film, and writing.

The devices for blurring contours are many. Impressionists are caught up in the transitoriness of all things. The painter Monet, when painting Rouen cathedral, did not directly catch its gothic structure, but an air envelope of a certain density, through which the cathedral could be seen and by which its appearance was modified with every shift of light.

Debussy's "Submerged Cathedral," "Gardens in Rain," "Reflection in Water," "Clouds," and "The Sea" summarize themes and intentions of impressionist painters and writers to suggest objects which have neither function nor substance, and are only indirectly revealed to the beholder at a certain distance. For this reason, characters in an impressionist novel are usually just an evocation of airiness and of inconsequence. Since the definition of character is inseparable from a novel's plot, character cannot exist in a formless novel. The most solid characters, such as Frédéric and Mme. Arnoux of Flaubert's *L'Education Sentimentale*, Joyce's Stephen Dedalus, Virginia Woolf's Mrs. Ramsay, Rilke's Malte, and Gide's Nathanaël, seem at times to melt away into a mere atmosphere. Even when they are given sharp perceptions, their character remains enclosed in a sort of envelope, it comes rarely into contact with others, and remains isolated. Nothing seems to have weight, form, structure, figure, or determination. There is more stress on connotation than on denotation. Images of haze, rain, damp air, water, fog, mist, smoke, and rivers, therefore, predominate and convey the impression of distant vision through unity of color under specific light.[27] The protagonists often hear and see from a distance only, being barely able to do either, and the reader, then, is reduced to guessing and interpreting gestures and attitudes.

Seen at a distance, no object has any clear and detailed outlines, and thus, automatically, the subject itself is subordinated to the melodious effect of colors and sounds, which then can be used to evoke a particular mood. Through unity of color, tint and tone, blurred outlines, and vagueness of meaning, impressionist writers and painters achieve musical effects. Color, together with sound and light effects, creates harmony.

Harmony, the "musical tableau,"[28] as Jean Hytier describes it in speaking of Gide's *Les Nourritures Terrestres* and *Paludes*, is their ideal. Internal harmony has always been the distinctive quality of any work of art. With the impressionists, this harmony is created to unite light and image. Baudelaire comes to this conclusion when he realizes that harmony is the basis of color, depending on the reflection of light on the image to be presented. "L'harmonie est la base de la théorie de la couleur. La mélodie est l'unité dans la couleur, ou la couleur générale. La mélodie veut une conclusion; c'est un ensemble où tous les effets concourent à un effet général."[29] If the author creates a "musical tableau," then, of course, no solution of the story is needed, but only unity of effect, the major theme or idea creating a kind of pictorial music. Color and light provide the essential structure of the impressionist painting and literature: their unity is no longer created by linear contours but by color and light only.

It seems, then, that the impressionist writer's recording of the sensations of light is associated with the experience of distance, and remoteness. Each motive is treated as though it lay far, even unattainably removed from the reader, in half-dissolving shapes transformed by atmosphere, moods, and memories. The light playing over these shapes does not bring them near to us, but, on the contrary, removes them from us in the sense that it dissolves their contours.

Space, like time, has become a surrounding atmosphere which cannot be measured or analyzed scientifically, only grasped intuitively, in a synthesis. It surrounds everything, and bounds nothing. Reality, for the impressionist, has become a vision of space, conceived as sensations of light and color. The unity of space and color sensation has been defined by Ernst Mach, in *Die Analyse der Empfindungen*, in 1885, as an interplay of the individual's consciousness and the surrounding world. Space is defined as the relationships which pieces of matter, in our experience, have with one another. Time, also, is the relationship between different occasions, again within the experience of the individual. In this allusive space and time, both human mind and physical objects have exactly the same ingredients, which from the point of view of psychology are sensations, and from the point of view of physics, the constituents of things. Mach calls spaces and times as appropriately sensations as colors and sounds. With him and the impressionists, the antithesis of ego and world, sensation and thing vanishes. All that exists is in contact with everything else. The German critic, Hermann Bahr, calls Mach's views the "philosophy of impressionism": "Alle Trennungen sind hier aufgehoben, das Physikalische und das Psychologische rinnt zusammen, Element und Empfindung sind eins, das Ich löst sich auf und alles ist nur eine ewige Flut, die hier zu stocken scheint, dort eiliger fliesst, alles ist nur Bewegung von Farben, Tönen, Wärmen, Drücken, Räumen und Zeiten, die auf der anderen Seite, bei uns herüben, als Stimmungen, Gefühle und Willen erscheinen. . . . es dauert vielleicht gar nicht lange und man nennt die Weltanschauung Machs einfach die 'Philosophie des Impressionismus.' "[30]

In impressionist literature, space is qualified by light, the signature of time. The reader is intended to seize the works of Flaubert, Proust, James, Pound, Joyce, and Mansfield spatially[31] in a moment of time, rather than as a time sequence. Time seems to be abolished; people, words, and gestures seem to be the elements of the same atmosphere; characters themselves are presented as static figures perceived at a certain distance. The self of these protagonists is not simply split, as with the romantics: it is atomized, with the impressionists, in the same way as light has dissolved the solidity of matter. The many expressions which convey this dissolution of the self can hardly be translated into English, as we read them in the works of Flaubert, Gide, Proust, Robbe-Grillet: *anéantissement du moi, abandon de soi; vase clos et sans communication; désagrégation, déperdition, épuisment; dépersonnalisation, dissolution;* the very essence of the human being seems to be dissolved in light.

CHAPTER THREE

The Play With Reflections

". . . character has distinct existence only in the ca-
pacity of an object of knowledge for the Other. Consciousness does not know its own character—unless in
determining itself reflectively from the standpoint of
another's point of view. . . . This is why pure introspective self-description does not give us character.
Proust's hero 'does not have' a directly apprehensible
character. . . ."

J.-P. Sartre, *Being and Nothingness*

1. The Journal, Diary, or Notebook

With the exception of Flaubert's work, all the books to be discussed here as illustrations of impressionist tendencies are either
diaries, notebooks, or *mémoires*. It is a commonplace among
critics to acknowledge the *Journal* of the Goncourts as the
manifesto of impressionist prose, much more so than their
Manette Salomon. It has not yet been explained, though, why the
journal or short sketches lend themselves better than a long piece
of prose to the reflection of impressions.[1] Writers of diaries,
notebooks, and memoirs have the advantage of making everything proceed from a certain instant: according to the moment,
they can change writing styles, that is the manner of suggesting
reality; they can change points of view in order to capture the
most volatile moments of life together with nuances of color and
tone, and to seize in passing the variations in aspect which the
same scene assumes at different moments; they can reveal the
development of awareness of the protagonist.

The great emphasis is on time. *La vision instantanée,* "instantaneous vision," of the authors discussed here gives us the impression of an infinity of universes which come into form, and show objects, places and events for as brief a span of time as human consciousness lends them its lucidity. Plotless sketches, with flashes of mood and place which are created and destroyed almost simultaneously, recall Joyce's *epiphanies.*

Impressionist prose seems to be an exercise in discontinuity. The traditional stable world is dissolved into the unfinished, the fragmentary. Ortega y Gasset recognizes the attempt of impressionist writers and artists to retain the spontaneous energy of a sketch in a finished painting or a piece of writing. Impressionist writers have found a way to write prose which is not bounded by a beginning and an end. It is not colored by any finality:

> A novelist must proceed in the same way as the impressionist painters who set down on canvas such elements as the spectator needs for seeing an apple, and leave it to him to give this material the finishing touches. Hence the fresh taste of all impressionistic painting. We seem to see the objects of a picture in a perpetual *status nascendi.* In the career of everything there are two moments of supreme drama: birth and death—*status nascens* and *status evanescens.* Nonimpressionistic painting, superior though it may be in other respects, suffers from one shortcoming: that it represents its objects altogether finished, mummified and, as it were, past. That actuality, that existence in the present tense, which things possess in impressionistic pictures is irremmediably missing.[2]

Baudelaire summarizes the common attempt of the impressionists to reject finite matter, and to give preference to the unfinished, the fragmentary. Speaking of Corot, Baudelaire says in "Salon de 1845": ". . . il y a une grande différence entre un morceau fait et un morceau fini . . . en général ce qui est *fait* n'est pas fini, et . . . une chose très finie peut n'être pas faite du tout. . . ."[3]

In Rimbaud's *Illuminations,* no one setting remains, no one character lives for long. The poetic universe destroys and creates almost simultaneously. Emotions dissolve into other emotions. In Gide's *Les Nourritures Terrestres,* the cities of Florence and Rome are perceived momentarily but immediately fade away, dissolved in light. "Colline de Vincigliata. Là j'ai vu pour la première fois les nuages, dans l'azur, se dissoudre; je m'en étonnai beaucoup ne pensant pas qu'ils pussent ainsi se résorber dans le ciel, croyant qu'ils duraient jusqu'à la pluie et ne pouvaient que s'épaissir. Mais non: j'en observais tous les flocons un à un disparaître; il ne restait plus que de l'azur. C'était une mort merveilleuse; un évanouissement en plein ciel."[4] Sartre begins *La Nausée* in the middle of things as Roquentin writes: "Le mieux serait d'écrire les événements au jour le jour." ("The best thing would be to write down events from day to day.") It is as if we had caught him in the middle of thought. And he ends the work in a state of flux, a moment of indecision which is no ending at all, but only a moment caught in passing. Proust opens *Du côté de Swann* with Marcel's awakening in a dark room, and offers no conclusion but the one that all reality is in a state of passing "and houses, roads, avenues are all fugitive, alas as the years."

The journal permits great changes in perspective, both in the narrator's view of his world and in our view of him. This means, sometimes, that the protagonists are seen and interpreted through other protagonists using the disappearing narrator of Flaubert, the double "I" of Proust, the *Je-Néant* or "absent I" of *La Jalousie,* or the many selves revealed by Rilke's Malte and Dazai's Yozo. Sometimes there is only a recording consciousness or an absorbing eye: its only identity in Robbe-Grillet's *La Jalousie* is that this eye belongs to a husband who is a plantation owner. Any indirection as to perspective conveys the many-sidedness of life, and the impressions of volatile, scurrying moments.

Why does the observer, whose personality is carefully withheld and who never expresses a judgment (Flaubert, Joyce, Proust, Sartre, Rilke, Osamu) attempt by every means to approach his protagonists and their surrounding worlds from many sides, as closely as human capabilities of perception and expression allow? Gide's protagonist Edouard, in *Les Faux-Monnayeurs,*

offers an answer to this question, rejecting the naturalist school
that always cuts its slices in the same direction, in time, lengthwise.[5] Edouard implies the durational as an integral mode of the
apprehension of reality, as contrasted with a spatial rendering of
life in fiction; for in the latter, time projected lengthwise is
nothing but space. Gide also explained his new viewpoint to
Roger Martin du Gard who recalls the following conversation
with Gide:

> "There you have your *Barois* and your *Thibault*. . . . You im-
> agine the biography of your main character, or the fortunes
> of your family, and you shine your light upon the subject,
> year by year, as best you can. . . . But now this is how I set
> about the *Faux-Monnayeurs*. . . ." He turns the page over,
> traces a big semicircle upon it, puts the torch in the middle,
> and revolves it in such a way that the light follows the semi-
> circular line while the torch itself never leaves the center
> of the page . . . These are two different aesthetic systems.
> You set out your facts, like a historian, in chronological or-
> der. Your book is like a panorama that unrolls itself before
> the reader. You never describe the past through the inter-
> mediary of a character who had no part in the incident.
> You never show us things seen from the side, or from a sur-
> prising or anachronistic point of view.[6]

As early as with Flaubert, an important innovation has taken
place: to present the protagonists and their world from many
viewpoints and in successive instants as fragmentary and progressive portraits, created by the pointillist perception of their
reader. Emma Bovary is systematically shown to us from the
outside, from Charles's viewpoint; but then, what had been subject becomes object, and the center of consciousness passes from
Charles to Emma, giving us a subjective vision of the character
in perspective. Proust, in depicting "Les clochers de Martinville,"
subordinates the exterior aspect of the landscape to Marcel's
own profound impression. When describing Saint-Hilaire, he is
not so much concerned with what time has done to the church,

but rather with what the church has done with time. He makes a geometrical use of time, and the church of Saint-Hilaire emerges as a citizen alongside Combray, a citizen with the self-consciousness of a living being.

Proust, fascinated by the impressionist painters' ability to arrest for all time a luminous instant of life, fills this instant with a kaleidoscope of exotic colors and odors, sounds, and perfumes. Thus, he exclaims, using the stylistic device of the metaphor, in *A la Recherche du Temps Perdu*, that an hour is not merely an hour, but it is a vase filled with perfumes, sounds, and climates. A metaphor, as these examples show, is for Proust the equivalent of sensation; the metaphorical equivalent of sensation is a perception.[7] For Proust's Marcel, for instance, the renewed sensory impression called forth by the taste of a cup of tea, provides a material bridge between the past and the present, and with it the world of Combray comes springing back to life in all its original freshness. For Proust, in the tradition of Bergson, it seems that it is in memory, above all, that duration exhibits itself, for in memory the past survives in the present. Metaphor is for Proust the major means of expressing the harmony of his world in a specific style as he explains in *Le Temps Retrouvé*:

> Une heure n'est pas qu'une heure, c'est un vase rempli de parfums, de sons, de projets et de climats. Ce que nous appelons la réalité est un certain rapport entre ces sensations et ces souvenirs qui nous entourent simultanément . . . la vérité ne commencera qu'au moment où l'écrivain prendra deux objets différents, posera leur rapport, analogue dans le monde de l'art à celui qu'est le rapport unique de la loi causale dans le monde de la science, et les enfermera dans les anneaux nécessaires d'un beau style; même, ainsi que la vie, quand en rapprochant une qualité commune à deux sensations, il dégagera leur essence commune en les réunissant l'une et l'autre pour les soustraire aux contingences du temps, dans une métaphore.[8]

In complete opposition to this view is the journal of Roquentin. His day to day report puts great emphasis on time; that is on regular "clock time." He twists and distorts it until the linear "clock time" loses all meaning and time becomes the great void in which *we* live. It does not run continually past us, but invades our being. Roquentin loses the sense of the "irreversibility of time." He explains that he cannot distinguish present from future, and realizes "the past did not exist." Time without future and past has no meaning as a measurement, and thus Roquentin is living in a world which is simply surrounded by time, in the same way that one may be surrounded by a cloud. This is time which plays upon surfaces, transforms things, yet measures nothing; and the world begins to disintegrate through the dissolution of clock time, through the erosion of the definiteness of objects. The disintegration of these familiar landmarks by which man orders his life goes much further than the realm of time and objects. It extends into the realm of space as well. Roquentin can no longer get his bearings by a visual or psychological measuring of space between him and an object, nor by the stability of the world around him.

Sartre's journal permits the return of Roquentin to the same incident, although each time the incident is colored somewhat differently by his state of mind and by his mood. For instance, we see the pebble incident through Roquentin's eyes: first without any comprehension of what has happened, later as he gains some measure of understanding; first as a nausea of the hands, and later as a sign of a more pervasive malaise, the first of many other nauseas.

Yozo's notebooks in *No Longer Human* are the last outreachings of a pathetic being toward his fellow men. At the time of their composition, Yozo was in a state of complete personality disintegration. The rhythm in the notebooks is created by Yozo's efforts at self reform. These are always followed by further degradation and more complete disintegration. This pattern of resurgence and further disintegration, recalling Stephen's efforts in *A Portrait of the Artist,* is repeated several times. Each cycle leaves Yozo more completely disintegrated than previously. The description of the three pictures of Yozo parallels the disintegration of his personality which we find in the notebooks. In the first picture, Yozo's face shows character, selfhood, and individuality. It is distinguishable from other faces, however, by its ugliness. The adjectives which the narrator uses in relation to the face evoke thoughts of the ugly horror of life: the face is "dreadful," "freakish," "unclean," "nauseating," "hideous." It is not the face of a human being, but of a "grinning monkey." In the second photograph, adjectives fail to describe the true horror of the picture. It lacks substance, weight, and humanity: "It is merely a blank sheet of paper, light as a feather, and it is smiling." Like a mask, the face seems to have no connection to the real self which lies behind it; it is artificial. This artificiality reflects Yozo's increased alienation from himself. He has succeeded perfectly in presenting himself to the world as a clown whose real self is masked. But the adjectives fail in describing the horror of this second picture; for the third, no adjectives are necessary. There is nothing there, "no expression whatsoever."

These passages illustrate that through the ways in which the protagonists come to interpret their situations, we see them change. We see their personalities as ceaseless processes of becoming. We see them as one sees various self-portraits of an artist; the variety representing not one face, but the many faces of the same man. This multitude of Roquentins, Maltes, Marcels, and Yozos whom we see is indicative of their lack of unity. Their mind's ceaseless flux, jumping across all boundaries of time and space is in harmony with the restlessness of waves, the variability of colors in nature, or the flow of a river.

The new concept of time, to present action in anachronological order, has been enthusiastically seized upon by representatives of the *nouveau roman*. It is Robbe-Grillet's endeavor, too, to do away with mechanical clock time: "Pourquoi chercher à reconstituer le temps des horloges dans un récit qui ne s'inquiète que du temps humain? N'est-ce pas plus sage de penser à notre propre mémoire, qui n'est jamais chronologique."[9] Claude Simon, in *Le Vent*, following the evolution of the novel in reference to this new concept of time, presents protagonists who seem to be frozen into some thick substance, recalling the thick atmosphere in which Poe's protagonist, Usher, moves. There is only a feeling of constant reiteration. Claude Simon presents a kind of image of the living dead in *L'Herbe,* a book in which nothing emerges clearly at first, except the haunting rhythms of the shivers of a paralyzed old person in agony. The protagonists move, autonomous and enclosed, isolated from one another, merging slowly within cascades of interminable sentences and an infinite number of parentheses, conveying a sense of the repulsiveness of all human beings. Time again has taken the dimension of space, and surrounds the individuals with atmosphere like a cloud which got stuck on a mountain.

In impressionist literature, the relationship of the individual to the surrounding world is re-evaluated. There is a new manner of feeling and taking part in the life of things, since existence is a going out toward primitive experience, which is fragmented into its sensational instants, and a return toward the interior of the self. In some cases these experiences and these instances relate to the past, often they do not. What all impressionist works have in common, however, is to give time the character of space, to impose spatial relations on time, to do away with a chronological narrative and replace it with sketches as used in journals, notebooks, and memoirs. The journal, notebook, and memoir forms allow these writers great freedom as to style and structure, as well as plot and character presentation.

In conclusion, we would like to quote a passage of 1893 in which André Gide tries to explain the deep significance of the journal in his own life and its application to his work; it also explains the endeavor of impressionist writers to present protagonists who are but reflections of the author at one particular instant of their lives. In Proust's *A la Recherche du Temps Perdu,* and, in Gide's *Les Faux-Monnayeurs,* i.e., the chief character is writing a novel that turns out to be the very novel we are reading. Both painters and writers have been tempted by a retroaction of the subject on itself which Gide calls a *"mise en abyme"*:

In a work of art I [Gide] rather like to find transposed, on the scale of the characters, the very subject of that work. Nothing throws a clearer light upon it or more surely establishes the proportions of the whole. Thus, in certain paintings of Memling or Quentin Metzys a small convex and dark mirror reflects the interior of the room in which the scene of the painting is taking place. . . . Finally, in literature, in the play scene in *Hamlet*, and elsewhere in many other plays. In *Wilhelm Meister* the scenes of the puppets or the celebration at the castle. In *The Fall of the House of Usher* the story that is read by Roderick, etc. None of these examples is altogether exact. What would be much more so, and would explain much better what I strove for in my *Cahiers*, in my Narcisse, and in the *Tentative*, is a comparison with the device of heraldry that consists in setting in the escutcheon a smaller one "*en abyme*," at the heart-point.[10]

This *mise en abyme*, this play with reflections, is the very essence of the impressionist prose of the *nouveau roman*. It means that the pattern of the whole is reflected or mirrored in certain of its parts. The author's narration in the first person makes it his own objectification of himself. The interpreter and the performer are the same person. This means, for instance, when an orchestra interprets a musical composition, the performance is incomplete until the performance is heard by some audience. The *mise en abyme* has several functions: it serves as a mirror of the major theme, of the narrator's self, and of the whole work. Each function serves "the play within the play" which Gide praised in *Hamlet* and in "The Fall of the House of Usher." Two worlds are in turn mirrored in each other.

2. *Impressionist Anti-Heroes*

The impressionist writer celebrates the union of the protagonist with the world. Strangely enough, this union is consummated by vision and not by participation. Vision elicits a choice between remaining passive or becoming active, as Hermann Bahr points out: "Sehen ist zugleich ein Leiden und ein Handeln."[11]

Impressionist protagonists are all passive. They passively undergo the basic dichotomy of life: with the vitalist Dilthey or with Baudelaire and Renoir, they may love "les choses où le son se mêle à la lumière[12] or with the nihilists on the contrary, more often in literature than in painting, they may be led inevitably to disaster, succumbing to their despair, imprisoned in a vision of loneliness, heaviness, and enclosure.

Their states of consciousness are waxing and waning, interpenetrating one another. They see images which arise for an instant, and then disappear. What remains is nothing but the sensation of contact with the object. Individuals seem to move, autonomous and enclosed, inside a system in which they attract, repel, and strike one another, without any fixed position. Their loss of a personal center (*Zerstreutheit*) and their consequent imperilment in a world of unconvincing vital relationships make them passive victims: "Der Impressionist kennt keine zeitliche, geschichtliche Tiefe, in der der Mensch Halt finden könnte,"[13] as Sommerhalder states; this is the very characteristic of Gide's Nathanaël. Detachment (*dénuement*) is the central mood of Gide's *Les Caves du Vatican* and *Les Nourritures Terrestres*: *Disponible* means to remain "uncommitted" to any particular experience, physical or spiritual. True happiness is for Nathanaël a state of fervent passivity. The self, then, seems to be bounded by no limits, defended by no frontiers, constituted by no definition: "suffocations; regonflements; rechutes.—Inertie de moi: qu'y suis-je?—Un bouchon—un pauvre bouchon sur les flots. Abandon à l'oubli des vagues; volupté du renoncement, être une chose."[14]

As in impressionist painting, where there is no color peculiar to any particular object, the protagonists in impressionist literature lack a composed personality. It seems that human life is broken up into fragments at will, and that the person is reduced to a discontinuous series of states. Whatever the protagonist perceives has no drama in it. The absence of drama implies the absence of plot. Gide says of his characters: "It may seem that I did not know how to make them come alive because I so readily gave them up as soon as their outline was sufficiently sketched."[15]

Impressionism means instantism. In *Les Nourritures Terrestres* life is reduced to instants. Instants are discontinuous, and life is an instantaneous experience. The self is discontinuous too: each new instant is lived in a new self, not committed to anything, yet always *disponible*. The deliberate sketchiness of Gide's characters, such as Ménalque or Nathanaël, finds its counterpart in impressionist painting. There is not much interest in human beings; this detachment from the human character is a stylistic device.[16] Recall that Poe's aesthetics, impressionist music, poetry, and painting are ordered to the illustration of a mood, a mood sometimes announced in the title. The so-called characters are only pretext.

Basically, there are two types of impressionist protagonists, the first reflecting their joy of life, such as Gide's Narcissus, in *Les Nourritures Terrestres*. Nathanaël and Ménalque are the two roles of Narcissus: the one who looks and the one who is seen. The act of seeing is more important than the thing seen. All obstacles standing in Narcissus' way are being removed, above all that former conception of moral values which seems to be incompatible with happiness for the individual. The original self, unhampered by social traditions and moral codes, is the only value. On the other hand, the protagonists of Flaubert, Sartre, Joyce, Dazai Osamu, and Rilke are at their best during those moments when their voices fade away to become hardly distinguishable from other distant sounds, during moments of physical and spiritual disintegration and collapse.

At this stage they join Gide's Narcissus: the flickering, unstable semi-transparent moment-to-moment being of consciousness, the shifting way in which it conceives objects and itself, ends in dissolution: "Pour la sensibilité nouvelle la vie est une profondeur trouble où la lumière de la conscience miroite seulement, se diffracte et s'épanouit avant de se perdre, comme les rayons du soleil lentement diffusés, puis absorbés dans l'eau, jusqu'à la cécité des profondeurs."[17] The states of the protagonist's consciousness find reflection in the images of drowning, sinking, intoxication, immobility, silence, dissolution, and decay. Immobility, universal silence, failure, inertia, paralysis (*étourdissement*), and unfulfilled dreams are in harmony with the structure of works based on the circular and repetitive themes of motion, stasis, and erosion.

L'Education Sentimentale, Dubliners, A Portrait of the Artist, Les Chemins de la Liberté, La Nausée, and *No Longer Human* seem to be conceived under the ambiguous sign of stasis and motion, of fall and flight, in response to their protagonists' contradictory needs to escape their solipsist selves and yet seek refuge in order to dissolve within it. Sooner or later, all protagonists dissolve into *la matière*, into what Sartre calls viscousness of existence and proliferation of matter. Abandonment to certain impressions leads to a renunciation of Frédéric's, Roquentin's, Stephen's, and Yozo's personalities. Frédéric passively surrenders to these drifting experiences. This allurement of nothingness and this yearning for annihilation are in harmony with the breakdown of the surrounding world; this is Frédéric's experience in *L'Education Sentimentale*: "C'était comme des parties de son coeur qui s'en allaient avec ces choses: et la monotonie des mêmes voix, des mêmes gestes l'engourdissait de fatigue, lui causait une torpeur funèbre, une dissolution."[18] Flaubert, in his correspondence, speaks of a similar experience, with the distinction that he is aware of his state of being: "Je ne crois pas même à moi, je ne sais pas si je suis bête ou spirituel, bon ou mauvais, avare ou prodigue. Comme tout le monde *je flotte entre tout cela*. Mon mérite est peut-être de m'en apercevoir et mon défaut d'avoir la franchise de le dire. D'ailleurs, est-on sûr de soi? Est-on sûr de ce qu'on pense, de ce qu'on sent?"[19] As early as with Flaubert, the solid vault of reality seems to have collapsed and a dizzying infinite opens up. What is called into question is the value of both the world of appearances and the self.

Malte realizes that most people after forty lose their authentic being:

Andere Leute setzen unheimlich schnell ihre Gesichter auf, eins nach dem andern, und tragen sie ab. Es scheint ihnen zuerst, sie hätten für immer, aber sie sind kaum vierzig; da ist schon das letzte. Das hat natürlich seine Tragik. Sie sind nicht gewohnt, Gesichter zu schonen, ihr letztes ist in acht Tagen durch, hat Löcher, ist an vielen Stellen dünn wie Papier, und da kommt dann nach und nach die Unterlage heraus, das Nichtgesicht, und sie gehen damit herum.[20]

Leo Spitzer quotes a similar experience of the "Anti-Intellektualist" and "Emotivist" Barrès speaking of Germans: "L'intelligence quelle petite chose à la surface de nous-mêmes! Certains Allemands ne disent pas 'je pense,' mais 'il pense en moi'; profondément, nous sommes des êtres affectifs."[21]

At the early stages of their experience, the impressionists seem to be rather optimistic about their becoming a sensitive slate on which impressions would be written without their volitional effort. Such a case is Rimbaud. Indeed, he is successful in his endeavor to arrive at the unknown through the disordering of all the senses. He exclaims: "C'est faux de dire: Je pense. On devrait dire: On me pense. . . . Car Je est un autre. . . . Cela m'est évident: j'assiste à l'éclosion de ma pensée: je la regarde, je l'écoute: je lance un coup d'archet: la symphonie fait son remuement dans les profondeurs, ou vient d'un bond sur la scène."[22] Thus, in his *Illuminations,* all man's stable framework and bounds are crumbling away like Poe's Usher and his house, overcome by dizziness.

At another stage, all the links of the protagonist with society, friendship or love, politics or ambition, share this chronic deterioration and devaluation. Disgust, inertia, erosion, decay, boredom, inaction, immobility, monotonous fixedness of time and motionless objects, and the opaque presence of beings that *are there* lead Emma Bovary's and Frédéric's consciousness, long before Sartre, to awareness of their superfluity. Emma and Frédéric share with Roquentin the feeling of senselessness, of insignificance, and of the fragmentariness of external experience.

In his novels, Sartre has repeatedly tried to show that all of us are superfluous, and that nobody is really necessary. His detachment goes so far as to reject all given, constituted values as limitations on our liberty. The breakdown of the control of reason, and of all the normal restraints which Roquentin experiences, is a way of questioning the co-existence of his thoughts and his self: "Ma pensée, c'est *moi*: voilà pourquoi je ne peux pas m'arrêter. J'existe par ce que je pense . . . et je ne peux pas m'empêcher de penser."[23] In *La Mort dans l'Ame*, the defeated soldiers undergo a dissolution of their selves during which they have the impression that something is thinking in them, instead of their thinking themselves: "Nous sommes le rêve d'une vermine, nos pensées s'épaisissent, deviennent de moins en moins humaines; des pensées velues, pattues courent partout, sautent d'un être à l'autre: la vermine va se réveiller."[24] Thus, some of Sartre's protagonists allow their thoughts to think themselves within them without their controlling them. Boris, in *La Mort dans l'Ame*, can no longer say "I," for instance, and less "I think," because something thinks within him. Boris not only lets his "I" dissolve itself, he disintegrates socially; for renouncing his own self also means losing any tie with his people, both French and Russians. When Boris is asked why he replaces the personal *nous* by the synthetic and neutral expression *ils*, he has no true excuse: "Pourquoi dis-tu: *ils* ont fait ce qu'ils ont pu? Si tu te sentais Français, tu dirais *nous*."[25] Mallarmé reports a similar experience to his friend Cazalis in a letter on May 14, 1867, in which he tells him that he is now impersonal, no longer Stéphane, but an aptitude of the spiritual universe to perceive and develop itself by way of that which was his Self: "C'est t'apprendre que je suis maintenant impersonnel et non plus Stéphane que tu as connu,—mais une aptitude qu'a l'Univers spirituel à se voir et se développer, à travers ce qui fut moi."[26]

Man, as these examples show, is no longer seen as essentially one as in the tradition of Molière and Balzac. Baudelaire, in March, 1851, reveals with "Alcohol and Hashish as Means of Multiplying the Individuality," the very goal of the impressionists: the multiplication of the self. Rimbaud exclaims: "I is someone else," and Proust, Gide, and Rilke are equally convinced that he is many. All the protagonists are to some degree multiple personalities with multiple faces, seen at different periods of their lives, in different situations, by gossip and hearsay. When the protagonist of *Le Nourritures Terrestres* is alone in himself, he ceases being a single person. "Je suis peuplé,"[27] he exclaims, when he becomes aware of the multiple selves of his being. He is either expanding beyond his limits or plunging into dissolution: "Je ne sentais parfois plus à mon corps de limites; il se continuait plus loin; ou parfois, voluptueusement, devenait poreux comme un sucre; je fondais."[28]

In many instances the protagonists, having lost their lucid consciousness and their will to change the situation, are like Malte and Roquentin overcome by the presence of objects. It is not so much personal feeling that controls here, as cosmic feeling, a consciousness of great impersonal forces underlying the order of the universe: the world of objects which starts to move, becomes the expression of the deep apprehensions of the protagonists. At that moment, their attitudes turn away from impressionism; they withdraw in a universe of their own, in which nothing exists any longer save dizzy vortices of color, the expression of their fears and anxieties.

Standing in front of a mirror while wearing a costume and a mask, the child Malte finds himself overpowered by the mirror. In a diabolical fashion it controls his being. It masters him and he tells us: "ich verlor allen Sinn, ich fiel einfach aus. Eine Sekunde lang hatte ich eine unbeschreibliche, wehe und vergebliche Sehnsucht nach mir, dann war nur noch er: es war nichts ausser ihm."[29] All identity and unity are lost when he sees the masked being gesturing in the mirror. Finally he collapses before a group of laughing servants; voiceless with fear, he faints and is lost in the heap of clothes on the floor. On another occasion, Malte's involuntary sympathy is so great that he gives his strength and will power to the other person, being emptied himself in the process: walking behind a man with epilepsy, the man's struggle imperceptibly becomes Malte's struggle.[30] These examples illustrate that Malte neither fights nor defends himself, nor is he defeated; he is simply swallowed up by his eventless, hopeless life.

Roquentin, in Sartre's *La Nausée,* has no self-image: he is caught in a world where subject and object have merged to become one and the same. He feels himself a crab, or feels in himself the same raw existence which he observes in the world around him. He no longer touches objects, but they touch him. The subject is no longer primary and the object constant. Both change. Both partake of the same form of existence. We see Roquentin's physical being in disjointed glances. His face makes no sense to him. He gets trapped by the mirror. He can't pull away from it, and is nauseated by his own lack of distinction. In staring at his features he sees that there is nothing human left. There is so little of his face that he goes to sleep on his feet while looking at himself. His only strong feature is his red hair. It is the one show of strength which redeems him from total ineffectuality. Roquentin's inner being is much like his disjointed self-image. We see of him not more than Rodin would show of a face in "Man with a Broken Nose." His inner life is the composite of impressions of the world around him. It is not that exposure to people has robbed him of a self-image; it is simply that he never had one in the first place.

With the exception of Frédéric Moreau, the early impressionists' confrontation with things and with nature was so marked, so direct, and their love for them so passionate and unrestrained, that inevitably their joyful, optimistic attitude toward nature did not find satisfaction. Man, whose only guiding principles in life relate to "living fully," as illustrated by Gide's Narcissus, is led to a state of spiritual chaos and disintegration. The pantheist surrender of Sartre's protagonists to the endless flux of appearance leads to their downfall. Man becomes the mere accessory of nature with no claims to specific rights and privileges as long as he remains the anti-hero.

The anti-hero, as seen in the context of several impressionist literary works, is first of all one who stands outside of society. In many cases he is unique by virtue of heightened sensibilities (for instance Malte, Roquentin, Gide's Narcissus in *Les Nourritures Terrestres,* Yozo in *No Longer Human*). He is a spiritual exile who cannot be part of a society which is itself in a state of disintegration and decomposition. It follows that because he is spiritually alienated from his society, he is a *déraciné*, an individual without roots, going from one locale to another in search of something tangible. The anti-hero's introspective nature takes him away from what is coldly logical and intellectual. He is, instead, highly irrational and emotional. He is sensitive and open to all impressions without passing moral judgments as to which type of impressions he should reject or adhere to wholeheartedly. In this respect, the anti-hero is amoral; both good and evil are valid experiences. To a large extent, this amorality in his nature leads him to what is tantamount to self-destruction and annihilation. Directionless, open to both ugliness and beauty which surround him on all sides, he is led to what is absurd and meaningless in life. He is the victim of an environment which usually reflects the particular atmosphere of a given moment. He changes as the world around him changes. Worse, his heart is dead and empty with hopelessness, and thus annihilates everything which comes to it. His eye is no longer capable of holding a visual impression; it has become an exhausted, empty stare. His end is disillusionment and despair, because he is defeated by the presence of the surrounding world whose passive victim he is. He lives in a cage like Rilke's "Panther"; beyond the bars of the world of objects there is no world for him.

It seems, then, that with impressionism a new manner of feeling and taking part in the life of things has been initiated. The impressionists have become victims of their impressions: the radiant beauty of that phenomenal world which the early impressionists optimistically regarded as an adequate truth, disintegrates. Impressionist protagonists often feel helpless, hopeless; they feel a crippling of the will power and a fruitlessness of all effort. They are so swallowed up by the routine of their uneventful, hopeless lives (such as Meursault, Malte) that they no longer come to discern a dissonance in their relationship between the world and their lives. Impressionist protagonists have sacrificed the most precious parts of their own self: lucidity and will. Their initial urge to live life fully destroys personality even as it exalts it.

CHAPTER FOUR

Stylistic Devices

". . . le style pour l'écrivain, aussi bien que la couleur pour le peintre, est une question non de technique mais de vision. . . ."

Marcel Proust, *Le Temps Retrouvé*, p. 256

("style for the writer, no less than color for the painter, is a question not of technique but of vision. . . .")

The question might be asked whether literary impressionism can be adequately defined as a style. There was never any literary impressionist manifesto.[1] In painting and music, evidently, impressionism is an acknowledged style. An impressionist artist, such as Monet confronting the cathedral of Rouen in 1894, paints it at different times of the day and under changing conditions of weather. Having a new slant on reality, he does not wish to represent facts about gothic style. He uses the cathedral as a means of suggesting a harmony of color and light, and an atmosphere at a certain moment of the day. The coloration of the painting is "due to the juxtaposition of the luminous waves."[2] Also in Monet's "Londres, le Parlement, trouée de soleil dans le brouillard," "Vétheuil, soleil couchant," "La Seine à Port-Villez," "La Seine à Vétheuil," "Impression," "Mist," and Pissarro's "Ile Lacroix, Rouen—Effect of Fog"—all distinct forms merge with one another, fog or sunshine throwing an almost transparent veil over the motif. The few pronounced objects seem to pierce the softness of the atmosphere, asserting their substance in contrast to the enveloping haze, merging sea and land, sky and water into the same vibration of color and light. None of these canvases seem to be finished, for the elements of the view are no longer delineated by clear, concise drawing. What remains is only a study of light and color, executed by short brushstrokes, merging and fusing all elements with one another. The technical methods by which Monet, the foremost impressionist painter, obtained solar atmospheric effects have a close counterpart in both music and literature.

Words and images affect each other, and the part played by "reflections" is subtle but important. The vagueness in which Debussy veils any clear statement of formal construction and softens the expression of the emotions that inspired the composition, is in accord with Mallarmé's famous statement: "To name an object is to sacrifice three-quarters of the enjoyment of the poem, which comes from the guessing bit by bit. To suggest it, that is our dream." Gabriel Fauré's melodies such as "By the Water's Edge," "The Walled Garden," evoke sea, waves, wind, and clouds in effects of tone as the painter does it in effects of lights, tints and tone. In literature, tone is a harmony, the general effect of color with light and shade.

It is a critical commonplace[3] that Baudelaire's prose poems have initiated new concepts of the structure of prose in which melodic, harmonic, and rhythmic images create a new kind of sound patterns and relationships. Their aesthetics remind us of those pronounced by Poe, well aware of the fact that it is "in music, perhaps, that the soul most nearly attains the great end for which, when inspired by the Poetic Sentiment, it struggles, the creation of supernal Beauty."[4] After Delacroix's discovery, colors in painting and writing evoke moods having a musical quality that exists independently of the subject depicted. The following passage from Balzac's *Le Lys dans la Vallée* (1835) describes theoretically what Baudelaire, and especially the impressionist painters at a later date, tried to suggest and express indirectly, aiming through the unity of color, light, tint, and tone at musical effects. Music, as Balzac points out, does not merely communicate ideas, but conveys emotions enabling us to feel the harmony of this world. It seems that light has disintegrated into color whose vibrations and musical effects create a musical harmony among all objects of perception. The passage is still romantic, in a sense that each flower represents a thought, and the thought is more important than the flower. It is impressionistic, in a sense that the complexity of sensations create a "mood."

> . . . je pensai que les couleurs et les feuillages avaient une harmonie, une poésie qui se faisait jour dans l'entendement en charmant le regard, comme les phrases musicales réveillent mille souvenirs au fond des coeurs aimants et aimés. Si la couleur est la lumière organisée, ne doit-elle pas avoir un sens comme les combinaisons de l'air ont le leur? Aidé par Jacques et Madeleine, . . . j'entrepris . . . deux bouquets par lesquels j'essayai de peindre un sentiment. . . . Soit une longue allée de forêt semblable à quelque nef de cathédrale, où les arbres sont des piliers, où leurs branches forment les arceaux de la voûte, au bout de laquelle une clairière lointaine aux jours mélangés d'ombres ou nuancés par les teintes rouges du couchant point à travers les feuilles et montre comme les vitraux colorés d'un choeur plein d'oiseaux qui chantent. . . . Jetez sur ces tableaux, tantôt des torrents de soleil ruisselant comme des ondes nourrissantes, tantôt des amas de nuées grises alignées comme les rides au front d'un vieillard, tantôt les tons froids d'un ciel faiblement orangé, sillonné de bandes d'un bleu pâle; puis écoutez? vous entendrez d'indéfinissables harmonies au milieu d'un silence qui confond. . . . Mon Dieu, que cela est beau! Vous comprendrez cette délicieuse correspondance par le détail d'un bouquet. . . .[5]

Impressionist artists seek neither instruction nor edification: their art expresses their desire for beauty, capturing the complexities of mood through the unities of effect according to the aesthetics of their immediate precursor, Edgar Allan Poe. Sacrificing meaning to sensuous effect, his prose and poetry enunciate the concept of vagueness. Vagueness is a major quality of any impressionist art, even while retaining the vivacity of the original impression. Poe's first principles confirm this impressionist tendency to suggest an indefinite meaning as being quite distinct from that of the transcendentalists: "Two things are invariably required: first, some amount of complexity, or more properly, adaptation; and secondly, some amount of suggestiveness—some under-current, however indefinite, of meaning. It is this latter, in especial, which imparts to a work of art so much of that richness . . . which we are too fond of confounding with the idea. It is the excess of the suggested meaning—it is the rendering this the upper instead of the under-current of the theme—which turns into prose (and that of the very flattest kind) the so-called poetry of the so-called transcendentalists."[6]

Just as light has come to invade matter, so the mood of the subject has come to invade and to transform the object. And in this transformation of the object, we find that there is no longer a subject and an object. Imperceptible transitions and dissolutions of subject and object reduce them to homogeneity, to a state of immersion. The conventional link between motivation and action is absent as early as with Flaubert's *L'Education Sentimentale*. Here Frédéric, the protagonist, is on a vessel which at the outset is about to steam away. As the monotonous landscape is slowly gliding by, his impressions merge and fade away. One desire awakens a contradictory desire as he moves through life, suggesting his steady irresolution. In *La Tentation de Saint Antoine*, also by Flaubert, the fusion of man and nature parallels their dissolution as the critic Richard observes: "All the envelopes—mineral, vegetable, and animal—steadily lose their solidity, and from one disappearance to another the saint finally discovers himself before a totally undifferentiated substance."[7]

With the impressionist writers, the subject matter is reduced to the state of motif keeping the artisic creation in the state of sensation. The absence of subject or plot implies the absence of drama as Giraudoux puts it: *"Mais il n'y a pas de sujets, il n'y a que des thèmes."*[8] There is no story. Action is pretext, since the dramatic interest has no aesthetic value. In this connection we may ask, what is the major event of Sartre's *Les Chemins de la Liberté*, if not defeat? Is the crisis more important than what happens between events? Sartre sees the defeat of the soldiers, and this defeat he mirrors in both the language and the structure of the novel.

As early as with Flaubert, the impressionist writer's objective is to create a self-contained work of art that is its own form and substance: "What seems beautiful·to me [Flaubert] and what I should like to do is a book about nothing, a book with no exterior attachment . . . a book which would have almost no subject, or whose subject at least would be almost invisible, if that is possible."[9]

The distinction of subject and object breaks down, a fact noticed by Proust in the discussion of Flaubert's *L'Education Sentimentale*: "Les choses ont autant de vie que les hommes, car c'est le raisonnement qui assigne à tout phénomène visuel des causes extérieures, mais dans l'impression première que nous recevons cette cause n'est pas impliquée."[10] Proust speaks of an action "dont les protagonistes sont généralement des choses . . ," of people "qui dans cette vision continue ne sont plus que les choses, mais pas moins."[11] In *Madame Bovary* we are struck by great empty spaces between events, during which all movement is immobilized; still, we have the impression of fullness created out of silence and hollowness. Proust is one of the first critics to discover that Flaubert, in *L'Education Sentimentale,* replaces action by impression, thereby accomplishing a revolutionary innovation in the novel as art form. ". . . dans *L'Education Sentimentale* la révolution est accomplie, ce qui jusqu'à Flaubert était action devient impression."[12]

What is the meaning of this change from action to impression? Action often relates to revolutionary political events in which impressionist writers are not interested at all. More important for them is to reveal what is lyrical in art and life. Among all the arts, it is music which naturally lends itself to transmutation and to the creation of moods. Listening to an opera, we might realize that it is music which permits speech to be understood: phenomenologically, music is anterior to spoken language; consciousness and mastery of a particular pitch of sound and of a particular rhythm precede the pronunciation of a word. Music does not present phenomena or objects directly, but fuses them into a kind of musical mood. Transmutation in music often takes the form of a succession of themes. One theme fades into another and later reappears; with each reappearance it takes on a slightly different character, though it is still easily recognizable.

How does the language of the impressionist writer reflect dominion of the passing mood over the permanent qualities of life? In literature, images are really visible. They may be clouded, their contours dimmed, but they are real: Gide, in *Les Nourritures Terrestres,* makes us both see and hear by its rhythm a similar waxing and waning of the image: "Je vois une génération qui monte, et je vois une génération qui descend. Je vois une énorme génération qui monte, qui monte tout armée de joie vers la vie."[13] Using words which are semantic as well as musical, Gide suggests a similar emergence and submersion of the image, embracing both man and nature in the same mood of appearing and disappearing:

> La lune parut entre les branches des chênes, monotone, mais belle autant que les autres fois. Par groupes, à présent ils causaient et je n'entendais que des phrases éparses; il me sembla que chacun parlait à tous les autres de l'amour et sans s'inquiéter s'il n'était par aucun autre écouté.
>
> Puis les conversations se défirent, et, comme la lune disparaissait derrière les branches plus épaisses des chênes, ils restèrent couchés les uns près des autres, dans les feuilles, écoutant sans plus les comprendre les parleurs ou les parleuses attardés, mais dont les voix plus discrètes ne parvinrent bientôt plus à nous que mêlées au chuchotement du ruisseau sur les mousses."[14]

The major purpose of his lyrical prose, Gide tells us, is to write not in French but in music, in *Les Cahiers d'André Walter*: "En Français? non, je voudrais écrire en musique."[15]

When Proust depicts a sunset near Honfleur, in *Les Plaisirs et les Jours,* a world of color, light, and music, of silence and noises, a world without any presentation, seems to move toward us for assimilation. He embodies self in it. The passage is like a dream in which sensations are freed from their sentimental and intellectual meaning. The world around the poet and in the poet seems to be both absent and present; the dream dematerializes nature, and the objects depicted seem to draw their existence from the vibrations of light without having any contours or volumes.

Tout d'un coup, un bruit léger s'éveilla longuement comme une inquiétude, rapidement grandit, sembla rouler sur le bois. C'était le frisson des feuilles froissées par la brise. Une à une je les entendais déferler comme des vagues sur le vaste silence de la nuit tout entière. Puis ce bruit même décrut et s'éteignit. Dans l'étroite prairie allongée devant moi entre les deux épaisses avenues de chênes, semblait couler un fleuve de clarté, contenu par ces deux quais d'ombre. La lumière de la lune, en évoquant la maison du garde, les feuillages, une voile, de la nuit où ils étaient anéanties, ne les avait pas réveillés. Dans ce silence de sommeil, elle n'éclairait que le vague fantôme de leur forme, sans qu'on pût distinguer les contours qui me les rendaient pendant le jour si réels, qui m'opprimaient de la certitude de leur présence et de la perpétuité de leur voisinage banal. La maison sans porte, le feuillage sans tronc, presque sans feuilles, la voile sans barque, semblaient, au lieu d'une réalité cruellement indéniable et monotonement habituelle, le rêve étrange, inconsistant et lumineux des arbres endormis qui plongeaient dans l'obscurité. . . . La seule réalité était dans cette irréelle lumière, et je l'invoquais en souriant. Je ne comprenais pas quelle mystérieuse ressemblance unissait mes peines aux solennels mystères qui se célébraient dans les bois, au ciel et sur la mer, je sentais que leur explication, leur consolation, leur pardon était proféré, et qu'il était sans importance que mon intelligence ne fût pas dans le secret, puisque mon coeur l'entendait si bien.[16]

Mood in the novel, light in painting, and whole tone scales in music indicate structural centers with perspectives constantly changing as the themes weave in and out of one another, sometimes blending, sometimes clashing, to form the pattern which is the impressionist work of art.

This method is further developed in the contemporary French novel. The emotional center, a kind of "objective correlative," in Robbe-Grillet's *La Jalousie,* is the crushing of a centipede against the wall, an act which is repeated at musical moments in significant variants throughout the novel. Isn't this book another realization of Flaubert's dream to create *un livre sur rien,* "a book about nothing"? When Claude Simon, who started his career as a painter, states his concept of the novel, we are struck by the fact that he, too, continues in the tradition of impressionist musicians, painters, and writers regarding theory and practice, style, language, and form:

> Quand je commence à écrire, je n'ai pas d'idées à communiquer. . . . au départ, j'essaie de trouver des équivalents verbaux à de vagues sensations. . . . A partir du moment où l'on n'entreprend plus de communiquer des idées qui préexisteraient à l'écriture, les choses se présentent tout autrement. Si j'écris: 'Il timbra la lettre,' c'est abstrait. Si au contraire je parle d'un timbre vert, du goût de la colle sur la langue qui le lèche, etc., aussitôt l'écriture devient 'sensorielle,' et, en quelque sorte, 'concrète'. . . . Une histoire continue telle qu'on la décrit dans le roman traditionnel, est artificiellement reconstituée; elle n'est ni perçue ni sentie.[17]

Sounds and sound patterns, as in impressionist music, are related to each other by arbitrary sensual aural criteria, doing away with punctuation (as did a predecessor, Joyce), in order to avoid any break in the organic and fluid growth of images. "Mais elle n'a rien, et personne ne la pleurera (et qu'est-ce la mort sans les pleurs?) sinon peut-être son frère, cet autre vieillard, et sans doute pas plus qu'elle ne se pleurerait elle-même, c'est-à-dire décent, qu'il est convenable de. . . ."[18] It would be impossible to quote Simon's extremely well-orchestrated sentences here, since they are made endless with elongated parentheses, recalling Proust. But the over-all harmony and the rhythm of Simon's work are all-important. The rhythmic phrase form, the dynamics, the articulation, and the tone color are basic in his work, as in any impressionist creation.

With the impressionist writers a new awareness sets in that a word does not express ideas, yet suggests a certain effect with an allusive vagueness in tone. Mallarmé in an often quoted passage, explains this new function of words to Degas: "Ce n'est pas avec des idées que l'on fait des vers . . . *c'est avec des mots.*" ("We do not write poetry with ideas, *but with words.*") This is a major quality of Nathalie Sarraute's "ultra-impressionnisme" as the critic Albérès points out: "C'est peut-être là le sujet du livre: l'écrivain occupé à jouer avec les mots au milieu de la rumeur confuse des hommes."[19]

Poe, Joyce, Rimbaud, and Mallarmé have initiated a movement in fiction to adapt changes of consciousness, of feelings or sensations, to the power of words, inventing a new language which by itself will be capable of expressing the multiple nuances of the personality and feelings. A word or an image placed in a particular context produces a particular effect. "The writer's work is a work of language rather than of thought" as Merleau-Ponty tells us in discussing Proust. "His task is to produce a system of signs whose internal articulation reproduces the contours of experience, the reliefs and sweeping lines of these contours in turn generate a syntax in depth, a mode of composition and recital which breaks the mold of the world and everyday language and refashions it."[20]

It might be surprising to know that even a philosopher such as Jean-Paul Sartre, in *La Nausée*, proceeds with stylistic devices that slowly dispense with all rational guidelines. While Roquentin, in *La Nausée,* is yet aware of what has happened to him, he writes in clear, reasonably concise sentences, using scientific terms: classify, determine, truth. These are hard, clear words which show clarity of purpose. But in the same entry of the diary, we have hints that there is an impending disintegration of the scientific, ordered world. There are no transitions between sentences or between paragraphs. There are sudden changes of intent. There is much use of passive verbs. Sentences begin with formless words: at least, anyhow. And the last sentence of this entry is so indecisive that it is left unfinished.[21] The uncertainty, the becoming, of this last phrase will be mirrored in the complete novel. Later in the novel, after Roquentin has refuted the use of reason, we see whole passages in which transitions are associational and where words, as well as sentences, are unfinished. All rational guidelines have disappeared. The line between the actual and the imagined has disintegrated.

In Joyce's *Dubliners* and *A Portrait of the Artist*, intellectual associations are completely dispensed with whenever Joyce wishes to capture the ephemeral, translucent atmosphere of Dublin.[22] Joyce seems to be going beyond form to seize, for a moment, the peculiarly sensual qualities of light playing havoc with the staid objects of the outside. In one passage, Stephen is journeying to Cork by the night mail train. His window is his frame on life, and outside objects flash by with kaleidoscopic effect, revealing only their essence in the repeated and momentary flaring up of tiny grains of fire. Joyce creates the impression of blurred images passing before his eyes in total silence by repetition of key words (flung), and by his use of the gerund and adjectival participles. Words take the place of objects: darkening, slipping, passing, glimmering, twinkling, etc. This blurring of images is an essential part of Joyce's technique, and so often his frame of reference is the window picture-frame, as with Flaubert who also used it with preference.

The methods of blurring contours are many. In Flaubert's work the use of the imperfect[23] allows us to enter *in medias res* in the mind of the protagonist. The imperfect suggests that something is to be but has not yet been accomplished: this is the impression of the first pages of *L'Education Sentimentale*:

> Le tumulte s'apaisait; tous avaient pris leur place; quelques-uns, debout, se chauffaient autour de la machine, et la cheminée crachait avec un râle lent et rythmique son panache de fumée noire; des gouttelettes de rosée coulaient sur les cuivres; le pont tremblait sous une petite vibration intérieure,

et les deux roues, tournant rapidement, battaient l'eau. . . .
La campagne était toute vide. Il y avait dans le ciel de petits
nuages blancs arrêtés,—et l'ennui, vaguement répandu, semblait alanguir la marche du bateau et rendre l'aspect des
voyageurs plus insignifiant encore.[24]

In *Les Chemins de la Liberté,* the imperfect conveys the somno-
lent, inconsistent existence of its protagonists who, in passively
undergoing a new situation, allow their lives to be dissolved into
nothingness, and who, like Frédéric Moreau, are immobile, sub-
missive and stifled, accepting the ineluctable flow of events; in
the same way that a boat keeps drifting on a river, they live on in
a state of drowsiness. The broken rhythm of their language confirms the absence of inner stability. Use of the imperfect also
raises the question of how the protagonists will react to the major
event: "La caravane s'était évanouie. Le silence et le vide à perte
de vue: un gouffre horizontal. Daniel était las: les rues ne me-
naient nulle part; sans les hommes, elles se ressemblaient toutes.
Le boulevard Saint-Michel, hier longue coulée d'or vers le sud,
c'était cette baleine crevée, le ventre en l'air."[25]

When Sartre depicts the disintegration of the protagonists'
selves, he conveys this dissolution in a rhythm of vague, intangi-
ble, and evanescent word effects. The images are vague, visual,
and audible. Repetition of key nouns is significant, and it works
to intensify and to transfigure the passage into a strange and
drowsy one in which aural effects take over the impressionist
painter's device of blurred colors and sights. We move with the
protagonists in an atmosphere of drowsiness and dreaminess. All
objective facts have vanished; almost everything stated appears
so by way of reflection in the consciousness of Schneider, the
protagonist in question:

Le visage disparaît et le rêve commence. L'ombre des barreaux glisse lentement sur le plancher, glisse et tourne sur le
corps à la renverse, escalade les caisses, tourne, tourne, pâlit,
la nuit monte le long du mur; à travers les barreaux, la lu-
carne semble une meurtrissure, une meurtrissure pâle, une

meurtrissure noire et puis, tout d'un coup, un oeil clair et gai, les barreaux reprennent leur ronde, ils tournent, l'ombre tourne comme un phare, la bête est en cage, des hommes s'agitent un moment puis disparaissent, le bateau dérive avec tous ces forçats morts de faim dans leurs cages. Une flamme d'allumette, un mot jaillit de la pénombre peint en lettres rouges, de biais, sur une des caisses: FRAGILE. . . . Fragile. Qu'est-ce qui est fragile? Nous sommes tous fragiles. Le goût, sur la langue, tourne, tourbillon solaire, un goût ancien, oublié, je m'étais oublié, *le fourmillement du soleil dans les feuilles des châtaigniers, la pluie de soleil sur mon front, je lisais dans le hamac, la maison blanche derrière moi, derrière moi la Touraine, j'aimais les arbres, le soleil et la maison, j'aimais le monde et le bonheur, oh! autrefois.* . . . Il retombe dans la sève gluante, dans la SUBJECTIVITÉ. . . .[26]

The qualities of images used by the writer, of color used by the painter, and of sound used by the musician seem to shade off into one another; thus, pitch almost functions as color, and color takes the place of line. In all impressionist creations, even in films, rhythm and color are inseparable and interdependent. Debussy's *Nuages* is a rendering in music of the immutable aspect of the sky, and of the slow, solemn motion of the lands, fading away in grey tones lightly tinged in white; in Whistler's painting, "Courbet à Trouville" (1865), sand, sea, and sky form "a harmony in blue and silver" whose effect is musical, the nuances of colors slowly fading away at the horizon; Courbet's "Calm Sea" (1869) conveys the majestic expanse of the sea, dotted here and there with brighter accents, yet at a distance losing all its objective content, suggesting the sense of absolute homogeneity among the different components that depict the moment.

A similar impression conveys the point of Antonioni's film, *The Red Desert.*[27] The woman protagonist is made a forlorn distant figure, merged in a heavy oppressive atmosphere by our consciousness of the coastline and the people around her. Her inner sorrow is made to seem less significant by her involvement in an exchange of commonplace remarks with the people around her.

These persons, as important as the world of objects, are presented when they momentarily establish some indefinable relationship with their surroundings. Antonioni does not care where they come from, where they are going, or what kind of people they are. Detachment is the key impression of the film. As do Renoir's early paintings, such as "A Day in the Country," it offers an experience of remoteness. In becoming aware of the way the earth stretches away before us toward the horizon, we, together with the woman protagonist, become aware of both the "distance" between our own act of existence and that of the objects we are looking at. To achieve distance is a stylistic device common to all impressionists, as Ortega y Gasset points out:

> The point of view has been retracted, has placed itself farther from the object, and we have passed from the proximate to the distant vision. . . . Between the eye and the bodies is interposed the most immediate object: hollow space, air. Floating in the air, transformed into chromatic gases, formless pennons, pure reflections, things have lost their solidity and contour. . . . Proximate vision dissociates, analyzes, distinguishes—it is feudal. Distant vision synthesizes, combines, throws together—it is democratic. The point of view becomes synopsis. The painting of bulk has been definitely transformed into the painting of hollow space.[28]

It seems, then, that impressionist artists are more attracted by water, sky, and sunsets than by people. A river is for the painter an animated surface of many colors. The river's intensity of tones, the reflection of color values, were favorite studies of impressionist painters,[29] musicians,[30] and writers. In literature, however, the water image is used less to sing the harmony of color and light than to be the basic connection between an initial emotional state and a final emotional state, controlling the protagonist as to his wishes and feelings. This image is most effective in *L'Education Sentimentale* and in Rimbaud's "Bateau Ivre." In both cases, the water's gliding motion carries away both the boat and the sentient mind of the protagonist into a distant world of faint outlines.

In Rimbaud's poem there is a willful confusion of sea and sky, giving the impression of limitless vastness; colors associated with the sunset and night evoke remote times and unpleasant sounds. The boat finally accepts its lot as the victim of a trap. Endless wanderings terminate in corruption, decay, despair, frustration, and senselessness, all of which are present as the major effect at the conclusion of the poem, recalling in theme and structure many a tale of E. A. Poe.

Sea and sky have formed for Whistler "a harmony in blue and silver." For Rimbaud and Proust they are coupled with images of land without any line of demarcation between them.[31] In Rimbaud's "Marine," light unites the two major impressions, coupled by memory and a present sensation, in a harmony of sound and color: the sea resembles a field, boats seem to be land-ploughs. The flat land is represented by currents (*courants*) whose eddies (*reflux*) describe ruts (*ornières*). Thus, Rimbaud superimposes an aquatic picture on flat land where the ploughs are ships, and the furrows are billows. A similar, often quoted distortion of reality is Proust's presentation of "Le Port de Carquethuit," in which he is extremely sensitive to the interpenetrability of all elements. Again, Proust uses urban terms to evoke the sea, marine terms to suggest the little town. These examples show that impressionism is a synthetic vision. Barriers of space no longer exist, since reality has no fixed structure for the impressionist. The meaning of an impressionist painting or of a piece of writing thus lies in an elaborate network of interrelated images, all of which reflect the "coloration," "mood," or "nuance" at which they are aiming.

Baudelaire's "Harmonie du Soir" and Laforgue's "Soir de Printemps sur le Boulevard" suggest in language and imagery a theme "où l'indécis au précis se joint"[32] ("where the indefinite joins the definite") and where words both paint and sing at once. All the olfactory, visual, and aural impressions of one moment flow together and form a synthesis of sense perceptions. In "Harmonie du Soir," the harmony of the whole arises from a delicately subtle development of the musical phrase in the rhythm of a waltz which turns into a swinging, undulating repetition of key images such as vibration, intoxication, coagulation, tomb, consume, and perfume; in opposing images of joy to those of darkness, a musical elegy[33] is suggested. Laforgue evokes the evening atmosphere in spring, the mood of a particular evening in spring, when he was the beholder of happy life in the boulevard. For this reason, the people in this passage caught his attention not for any personal quality (even the beholder uses the neutral impersonal *on*), but only as an integral part of a mood of the scene around him; the result is the reflection of a luminous *joie de vivre* such as Renoir presented so often, yet with the eye of an almost dispassionate observer. Color and light are used in the same rhythm when Renoir, for instance, depicted a happy afternoon in "La Grenouillère." Both language and imagery evoke the rhythm of dancers perceived from a distance and for short instants only. The great number of commas has its equivalent in the impressionist's broken brushstrokes. The passage illustrates at its best what Laforgue calls *la ligne brisée,*[34] which is so very characteristic of impressionist style.

SOIR DE PRINTEMPS SUR LES BOULEVARDS.—Un soir de printemps sur un banc, grands boulevards, près des Variétés. Un café ruisselant de gaz. Une cocotte toute en rouge allant de bock en bock. Au premier, tout sombre, recueilli, des lampes, des tables, des crânes penchés, un cabinet de lecture. Au second, éblouissement du gaz, toutes les fenêtres ouvertes, des fleurs, des parfums, un bal. On n'entend pas la musique dans le grand bruit qui monte de la chaussée grouillante de piétons et de fiacres avec les passages qui dévorent et vomissent sans cesse du monde et la criée du programme devant le péristyle des Variétés.— Mais on voit danser, le long de ces dix fenêtres, des hommes en frac noir, devant blanc, tournant en cadence, tenant une femme bleue, rose, lilas, blanche, la tenant à peine embrassée, très correctement, on les voit passer, repasser, sérieux, sans rire (on n'entend pas la musique qui les fait danser). Un groupe de souteneurs passe; l'un dit: "Mon cher, elle a fait dix francs."—Aux Variétés, une cohue sort pour l'entr'acte; et toujours l'enfer du boulevard, les fiacres, les cafés,

le gaz, les vitrines, toujours, des passants. Ces cocottes qui
passent sous les clartés crues des cafés.—Près de moi un
kiosque de journaux—deux femmes causent; l'une dit: "Pour
sûr, elle ne passera pas la nuit, et son môme qui a donné la
gale au mien." Les omnibus chargés des deux sexes tous
ayant leur soucis, leur fanges.
En haut les étoiles douces et éternelles.[35]

Impressionist writers depict the act of seeing. They follow
Gide's recommendation in *Les Nourritures Terrestres*: "Que
l'*importance* soit dans ton regard, non dans la chose regardée."[36]
Word order conforms to the order of perception, sometimes de-
laying the arrival of the subject to produce a *crescendo* effect.
Proust produces such an .effect of a stifling, charged atmosphere
by using present participles which give the sensation of immediacy and continuity. The fluid sounds of the adjectives, the broken
rhythm of each sentence, finally release the long expected dread,
the rain: "Un petit coup au carreau, comme si quelque chose
l'avait heurté, suivi d'une ample chute légère comme de grains
de sable qu'on eût laissé tomber d'une fenêtre au-dessus, puis la
chute s'étendant, se réglant, adoptant un rythme, devenant
fluide, sonore, musicale, innombrable, universelle: c'était la
pluie."[37] The atmosphere in which all things become liquid replaces here the old conception of space.

Sickness and death adopt, as Malte tells us, the characteristics
of the person it attacks. He contrasts personal death with a hos-
pital death where sickness becomes anonymous, and cannot
express the person. Thoughts of death fuse with the surroundings
of Malte's grandfather, Christoph Detlev, in harmony with the
broken rhythm of sentences which describe the fall of objects
and which lead to the major effect, the death of Chamberlain
Christoph Detlev Brigge; the repetition of key words suggests,
in ever louder and penetrating rhythm, death. The passage conveys the impression that death emerges from the world of broken
and falling objects as a necessity. Even structure and images reflect a "coloration" of death which penetrates and dissolves both
subject and object simultaneously. The crescendo of key words,

obtained by an elaborate arrangement of rhythms and images, creates the effect of a musical elegy. The predominant sound-effects excite our soul, conveying the impression that these sounds live.

Ja, es war für diese geistesabwesenden, verschlafenen Dinge eine schreckliche Zeit. Es passierte, dass aus Büchern, die irgend eine hastige Hand ungeschickt geöffnet hatte, Rosen-blätter heraustaumelten, die zertreten wurden; kleine, schwächliche Gegenstände wurden ergriffen und, nachdem sie sofort zerbrochen waren, schnell wieder hingelegt, man-ches Verbogene auch unter Vorhänge gesteckt oder gar hin-ter das goldene Netz des Kamingitters geworfen. Und von Zeit zu Zeit fiel etwas, fiel verhüllt auf Teppich, fiel hell auf das harte Parkett, aber es zerschlug da und dort, zersprang scharf oder brach fast lautlos auf, denn diese Dinge, ver-wöhnt wie sie waren, vertrugen keinerlei Fall. Und wäre es jemandem eingefallen zu fragen, was die Ursache von alledem sei, was über dieses ängstlich gehütete Zimmer alles Untergangs Fülle herabgerufen habe,—so hätte es nur *eine* Antwort gegeben: der Tod. Christoph Detlevs Tod lebte nun schon seit vielen, vielen Tagen auf Ulsgaard und redete mit allen und verlangte. Verlangte, getragen zu werden, verlangte das blaue Zimmer, verlangte den kleinen Salon, verlangte den Saal. Verlangte die Hunde, verlangte, dass man lache, spreche, spiele und still sei und alles zugleich. Verlangte Freunde zu sehen, Frauen and Verstorbene, und verlangte selber zu sterben: verlangte. Verlangte und schrie.[38]

These devices constantly remind us of Poe and Joyce's world, a world constituted by the power of words, where the world of appearance is broken up into fragments. Their protagonists dis-cover a certain significance in cracks, fissures, broken objects, cracked looking-glasses, ragged mountains, and crumbling houses. The appearance of these images of a broken world suggest that things fall apart, that "the center does not hold," and still there is an undefinable harmony created by the rhythmical effects of sound and color.

Conclusion

Impressionist writers have created a new vision of the world. With them, faith in an absolute has disappeared, the world has been relativized. The Cartesian tendency to divide up the world, to fix and determine it, to comprehend and classify, to recognize in the world things we already know, this conceptualization of the world is for the impressionist writer and artist an *objet-en-soi,* a "thing-in-itself," a reality with no possibility of growth, a dead world. Descartes used the sense of touch as a model for the visual act: an act of seeing could only be considered the occasion for thinking (*concevoir*) the object.

Impressionist writers begin with an empirical reality rather than an abstract idea. Reality, for the impressionists, has become a vision of space, conceived as sensations of light and color. Space is no longer a geometrical medium, but a medium of light which the impressionist artist can render by color, the impressionist writer by its equivalents: the atomization of color is accomplished by weak verbs (glisser, *paraître*), and auxiliaries (*avoir*), whereas the vibration of light is implied in the nouns (substantivized color adjectives, quality nouns, action nouns). Color also does not render depth, but atmosphere. Impressionist writers oppose irregularity and variety of sensations to the order of reason, being convinced that both in nature and in art all beauty is irregular.

The major effect of impressionist prose is lyrical, the writer being both Orion and Orpheus at once. This concept is as old as humanity: Augustine, in line with the whole of ancient authors included poetry under music. Nietzsche, in his *Birth of Tragedy,* declared the natural identity between the lyric poet and the musician; Poe wishes poetry to be the "Rhythmical Creation of Beauty," and Bergson has finally advanced the notion that melody is the type of artistic realization *par excellence,* because it flows on without a clearly defined succession. This is the basic conviction of Proust whose Vinteuil is the prototype of an impressionist musician, and of Verlaine whose "De la musique avant toute chose" sets the key note for all literary impressionist creations. What all impressionist writers wish to achieve is harmony, a rhythmical effect of beauty, stressing the autonomy of their creation. Their work reflects dominion of the passing mood over the permanent qualities of life. The sum total of these qualities of impressionist works seems to point to the same underlying forces which are evident in the ideas of the age: change, flux and instability, detachment. Scenes from the dynamic everyday world of speed and change are presented in the light of atmospheric color effects which, paradoxically, do not invite to action, but contemplation. Atmosphere lends the image a static quality. With an atmospheric theme nothing happens.

The common attitude of impressionist writers is a paradoxical one: by avoiding the pursuit of the ineffable, they actually reinstate the *human-cum senses* in the spectator or reader of their work, yet at the same time, through their use of the texture of light and color they create a harmony, a *Stimmung* (atmosphere, ambience, mood, if the German word is to be vaguely translated) referring both to the mood of a protagonist and to the unity of atmosphere adhering to a situation: thus, they seem to be detached from the human character who simply *is there*. The individual's consciousness fuses with the impressions from the outside world: outer and inner space becomes a single space of *Stimmung*. If the self is always becoming and never "is," in order not to get *figé*, "congealed," as Sartre would say, or *encrusté*, "encrusted," in Gide's words, in a world of transition and violent change, then all faith in individual identity and solidity is questioned. The multitude of Roquentins, Marcels, Maltes, and Yozos whom we see are indicative of their lack of unity.

The romantic themes of the relation of nature to God, and the relation of man's spirit to God and nature are no more relevant for individuals who question the purposive and harmonious order of the universe, its providential design. Impressionist literature deals with the psychology of the individual who is not only estranged from his social environment, but also alienated from himself. The individual's urge to live life at its fullest, paradoxically, ends in emptiness and destruction of the self. He cannot cope with the demands of a society which he feels demands that he wear masks and assume artificial poses in the presence of others. In a mechanized age, his world is neutral and impersonal. The dissolution of the individual's self is reflected as early as with Flaubert in expressions which can hardly be translated into any other language: *anéantissement; abandon; oubli; dénuement; dépouillement; désagrégation; déperdition; épuisment; dépersonnalisation; dissolution.*

We have found the first sustained use of impressionist techniques in *L'Education Sentimentale;* Flaubert's use of the *style indirect libre* anticipates the first *crise de conscience.* Since Flaubert, the essential tenet of all impressionist art is illusion. In summary, we have quoted passages from both poetry and prose, since we hold that the lyrical fiction is an outgrowth of both the aesthetics of Flaubert's prose and Baudelaire's prose poems. We found impressionist tendencies in certain poems of Verlaine and Rimbaud; in the critical statements of Laforgue and Mallarmé; in the early works of Gide, Rilke, Proust, and Sartre, and the very recent manifestations in the works of Robbe-Grillet, Nathalie Sarraute, and Claude Simon. All these various impressionist tendencies present an event in cultural history and result in a new reality of the novel. As Albérès observes: "La réalité du roman n'est plus à sa surface, mais dans ce qu'il ne parvient pas à formuler entièrement."[1]

Illustrations

EUGENE DELACROIX

"Cheval attaqué par une Lionne," 1844

We do not claim that literary impressionism was a matter of writers deliberately trying to transpose into their medium effects achieved in the other art forms. We may back-date the word "impressionism" to Flaubert, although it was invented after his time and was connected in the first instance with painting. As early as with Delacroix painting became a universe apart from human events and personalities. The art of Delacroix and impressionist writers creates illusions and does not transmit realities. He has recognized the possibilities of constructing with color, not simply with light and shade. Thus, he describes a system of color relationships based on Newtonian principles. These color relationships parallel the anachronological order of themes the writer uses in order to create the impression of the space-time continuum. With "Cheval attaqué par une Lionne" (1844) Delacroix creates an anatomous world of beautiful forms and colors, approaching the contours with a certain caution. Indeed, the contour seems to come last, the surface is fluid, and there is a spontaneity of effect, an overall unity of expression which dramatizes in a still romantic way the ferocity of the little lion. The painting, with its discontinuous and elusive contours, has the quality of a sketch which is the basic inspiration of both impressionist writers and painters.

JAMES McNEILL WHISTLER

"Portrait of the Artist's Mother; Arrangement in Grey and Black," 1872

Whistler's style still reveals traces of classicism with his simplicity of composition and serenity translated into static, balanced shapes. Omitting brilliant colors, he creates a harmony of tones based on the nuances of grey and black, shades which will be rejected by the impressionists. The picture is a harmony, a symphony, an arrangement. The monumental character of Mrs. Whistler's pose conveys classical calm in a restrained and dignified mood of repose. The composition is constructed on muted colors and on the indirect suggestions of the depth of Mrs. Whistler's personality. This tonal painting compares with his friend Mallarmé's fondness for alliteration; the tenets of their aesthetics are allusion and suggestion.

CAMILLE PISSARRO

"La diligence à Louveciennes," 1870

Flaubert's *L'Education Sentimentale,* Verlaine's *Art Poétique,* Baudelaire's *Petits poèmes en prose* appeared in 1868-72, precisely at the time when the earliest canvases painted in a recognizably impressionist style were being produced. Pissarro preserves the transitory character of the scene by the mastery of light and atmosphere. Each gleam of color is noted in the slightest variation of light and shadow. There appears a solid construction of space and a distinct feeling of structural solidity.

PIERRE AUGUSTE RENOIR

"La Grenouillère," 1869

Impressionism in painting has come to seem a symbol of a joyous, carefree attitude to life with both Renoir and Monet. How is it, then, that Flaubert was a somber impressionist *avant la lettre*, when the school of painters was remarkably cheerful with the exception of both Degas and Van Gogh? Impressionism, in all the arts, is a form of response to certain attitudes current from about 1870 onward: attitudes, that is, of skepticism toward all forms of transcendentalism, but equally toward all forms of rational intellectualism. With Renoir the happy mood of "La Grenouillère" achieves form: it calls not on memory but on a faculty of sensory impressionability. Thus, Renoir creates a lyrical harmony of light and color; the tones and contours are soft and filmy; with fresh and subtle tints he captures the ineffable beauty and delicacy of the young lady suggesting the impression of brightness and warmth.

CLAUDE MONET

"Régates à Argenteuil," 1872

Argenteuil on the Seine is a name closely associated
with impressionism. The color oscillation of blues, whites,
and reds induces the same sensuous pleasure as the arrangement of consonants and vowels in the poems of
Verlaine (1844-96) and Rimbaud (1856-91) with mu-
sical-pictorial moods in which sonorous words take the
function of colors. Monet presents both the water and the
clouds in a horizontal rhythm, in contrast to the vertical
darting of the white sails. As the colors are in juxtaposition and not held together by definitive lines, they give
the desired effect only if viewed from a certain distance.

CLAUDE MONET

"Femme à l'Ombrelle," 1886

Monet's light-hearted approach is deceptive, as his paintings are immediate precursors of the anguished compositions of Van Gogh, and of Degas' cruel analysis of human weaknesses. Indeed, beauty is born of an ephemeral association of the lady, a parasol and light, of light with its life-giving vitality. Monet achieves the effect of great luminosity full of lyricism. However, he indirectly expresses some pessimism; without sunlight there seems to be no beauty; and beauty can only be fleeting.

CLAUDE MONET

"La Cathédrale de Rouen — plein soleil," 1894

While Proust saw reality through the prism of memory, impressionist painters were at pains to forget what they knew so as to achieve the "impression" in its original freshness. A peak in Monet's materialization of the ephemeral is arrived at in the cathedrals, realizing the agonizing fact that nature is changing so rapidly at each moment. Therefore, he hopes to eternalize the instant. The picture is not the representation of the gothic Rouen cathedral, but rather of the atmosphere ,in which it is immersed. This atmosphere suggests a living fluid. The form of the cathedral can only be inferred from the differing intensities of light reflected from the surfaces which seem to be in dissolution.

EDGAR DEGAS

"Aux Courses: Jockeys amateurs près d'une voiture," 1879

Degas refused to be identified with the impressionists, yet most art critics give him the label of being an impressionist. Indeed, he expresses some tenets of impressionist theory. The colored silhouettes of the jockeys give the impression of immediacy: at the edge of the composition, horses, people, and the carriage are cut across in order to induce a sense of the space and to lead us into the painting. Thus, this painting suggests the movement and not the static quality of the jockeys. There are no strong defining lines, edges, or limits.

VINCENT VAN GOGH

"L'Eglise d'Auvers," 1890

Van Gogh, when starting to paint in the impressionist way, often and suddenly felt the inner necessity to express his emotions in colors independent from the object under consideration. Especially when painting the portrait of one of his artist friends, impressionist aesthetic problems have suddenly been replaced by pre-eminently human problems. At the end of his career his art has become a means of expressing his personal feelings: the colors used in painting "L'Eglise d'Auvers" are expressive of his personal emotions and express the artist's inmost self. Thus, he exteriorizes his reaction to the world. The church becomes a symbol of his wretched and disordered existence: it expresses not only his disillusionment and distress, his disenchantment and incurable melancholy, but also his sense of guilt. The intensity of color, the vigorous drawing, reflect the frenzy of his own nature before he shot himself. Thus, he no longer abandons himself to the external world, as did the impressionists, but concentrates on the expression of his inner world, a world of fear and anguish. Both space and objects suddenly start to move.

PAUL CEZANNE

"Nature Morte aux Oignons," 1888-90

Impressionism, as an artistic movement, had pretty well worked itself out by about 1886, whereas it is still a potent force in literature even today. Cézanne's classicism, as revealed in "Nature morte aux oignons," seems to be full of repressed Romanticism. He solidifies the visual appearances, and submits them to geometrical rules, in order to recapture the plastic and structural qualities of things. Thus, he is no longer interested in the most immediate and changeable aspects of things. Pictorial space excludes the notion of distance and depth. The forms of the *oignons*, the bottle, and the glass are arranged on a single vertical plane without any fragmentation of color. Thus, his mind organizes the sensation. It is a sensation of permanence rather than the passing effect of light.

Notes

Notes

Introduction

1. Jules Laforgue, *Oeuvres Complètes. Mélanges Posthumes*, "L'Art Impressionniste" (Paris: Mercure de France, 1903), pp. 176-177. "[a natural eye] . . . reaches a point where it can see reality in the living atmosphere of forms, decomposed, refracted, reflected by beings and things, in incessant vibration. Such is this first characteristic of the impressionistic eye."

2. Walter Melang, "Flaubert als Begründer des literarischen 'Impressionismus' in Frankreich," Dissertation (Emsdetten: Lechte, 1933), p. 10; Eugen Lerch, *Handbuch der Frankreichkunde* (Frankfurt: Moritz Diesterweg, 1930), p. 121; Harry Levin, *The Gates of Horn: A Study of Five French Realists* (New York: Oxford University Press, 1966), pp. 230-231. "The term 'impressionism' would not be current until 1874, when Monet exhibited his "Impression: soleil levant"; but members of that school were gathering at Batignolles when Flaubert published his book, and of them it constantly reminds us: of Pissarro, when Frédéric strolls down the boulevard; of Manet, when he joins his friends at a café; of Monet, when he glimpses reflections in the river; of Degas, when he takes Rosanette to the races; of Renoir, when he kneels at the feet of Mme Arnoux."

3. We shall not go into the details of *le style indirect libre*. The best studies on this question are Alf Lombard, *Les Constructions Nominales dans le Français moderne*, étude syntaxique et stylistique (Uppsala et Stockholm, n.d.) and Eugen Lerch, pp. 112-131.

4. André Gide, *Les Cahiers et les Poésies d'André Walter* (Paris: NRF Gallimard, 1952).

5. Rainer Maria Rilke et André Gide, *Correspondance 1909-1926* (Paris: Correa, 1952); Rainer M. Rilke, A. Gide et E. Verhaeren, *Correspondance inédite* (Paris: Ed. Messein, 1955).

6. Rainer Maria Rilke, "Les Cahiers de Malte Lauride Brigge" (fragments), *La Nouvelle Revue Française*, 1er juillet 1911.

7. K. A. Batterby, *Rilke and France, A Study in Poetic Development*, "Gide" (London: Oxford University Press, 1966), p. 133.

8. *Letters of Rainer Maria Rilke, 1892-1910*, translated by Jane Bannard Greene and M. D. Herter Norton (New York: W. W. Norton and Co., 1945).

9. *Letters of Rainer Maria Rilke 1892-1910*, pp. 314-316, October 19, 1907.

10. Roquentin explains this distinction between existence and being: for him the jazz melody does not *exist* but is–it is beyond the real world.

11. Eugene F. Kaelin, *An Existentialist Aesthetic, The Theories of Sartre and Merleau-Ponty* (Madison, Milwaukee, and London: The University of Wisconsin Press, 1966), pp. 395-397.

12. René Albérès, *Métamorphoses du roman* (Paris: Albin Michel, 1966); *Le roman d'aujourd'hui*, 1960-1970 (Paris: Albin Michel, 1970); "Aux sources du nouveau roman: L'impressionnisme anglais," *Revue de Paris*, LXIX (May 1962), pp. 74-86, etc.

13. Arnold Hauser, *The Social History of Art*, IV (New York: Vintage Books, 1960), pp. 166-225.

14. André Gide, *Les Faux-Monnayeurs* (Paris: Le Livre de Poche, 1925), p. 231. ("*L'état c'est moi!* I, the artist; civil or not, my work doesn't pretend to rival anything.")

15. Alain Robbe-Grillet, *Pour le nouveau roman* (Paris: NRF Gallimard, 1963) p. 152. ("We no longer believe in the starched, ready-made meanings that the old divine order, and afterwards the rationalist order of the 19th century, handed over to man; we transfer all our hope to man: the forms he creates can bring meaning to the world.")

Chapter One

1. Emile Littré, *Dictionnaire de la langue française* (Paris: Hachette, 1962), t. 4, p. 1815. ("The horror of the composition is the characteristic sign of impressionism. It spurns all effect obtained through intellectual and subjective affectations; it acknowledges only the free arrangements of nature.")

2. Ferdinand Brunetière, *Le Roman Naturaliste* (Paris: Lévy, 1893). ("We can already define literary impressionism as a systematic transposition of the expressive methods of art which is the art of writing.")

3. Hermann Bahr, *Zur Überwindung des Naturalismus*. Theoretische Schriften 1887-1904 (Stuttgart, Berlin, Köln, Mainz: Kohlhammer Verlag, 1968); *Kulturprofile der Jahrhundertwende* (Wien: H. Bauer, 1962), pp. 176-186; Joseph Warren Beach, *The Twentieth Century Novel* (New York: The Century Co., 1960); Jethro Bithell, *Modern German Literature, 1880-1950* (London: Methuen & Co., Ltd., 1959); Richard Hamann, *Der Impressionismus in Leben und Kunst* (Marburg: Kunstgeschichtliches Seminar, 1923); Ulrich Lauterbach, *Hermann Bang*, Studien zum dänischen Impressionismus (Breslau; Maruschke & Berendt, 1937); Viola Hopkins Winner, *Henry*

James and the Visual Arts (Charlottesville: The University Press of Virginia, 1970.)

4. Helmut A. Hatzfeld, *Literature through Art* (New York: Oxford University Press, 1952), p. 166; Walter Melang, "Flaubert als Begründer des literarischen Impressionismus in Frankreich," Dissertation (Emsdetten: Lechte, 1933), p. 81: Melang identifies impressionism with *äussersten Realismus*, "extreme realism."

5. Hermann Bahr, *Expressionismus* (München: Delphin Verlag, 1918), p. 67. ("Impressionism is merely the last stage of classical art, it is the completion and the culmination of classicism insofar as it seeks to increase outer vision to the highest extent, to exclude inner vision as much as possible, and steadily to decrease the role of the eye as an instrument directed by independent and spontaneous will, and thus to make man into a completely passive victim of his senses.")

6. Georg Loesch, "Die impressionistische Syntax der Goncourt (Eine syntaktisch-stylistische Untersuchung)" Dissertation (Nürnberg: Benedikt Hilz, 1919).

7. L. Desprez, *L'évolution naturaliste* (Paris: Tresse, 1884), p. 94 ff.

8. Paul Bourget, *Essais de psychologie contemporaine*, II, 1885, 135-193, does not use the term "impressionism," yet studies the style of the Goncourts and its parallels in impressionist painting; Beverly Jean Gibbs, "Impressionism as a Literary Movement," *Modern Language Journal*, 36 (1952), pp. 175-183; Jethro Bithell, *Modern German Literature, 1880-1950* (London: Methuen & Co., Ltd., 1950), "Cosmic Impressionists and Epic Infinites," pp. 242-250; "The Novel of Impressionism," pp. 279-320; Arnold Hauser, *The Social History of Art*, IV (New York: Vintage Books, 1951), p. 170.

9. Petit de Julleville, *Histoire de la langue et de la littérature Française, des origines à 1900*, Tome VIII (Paris: 1899), 183-184; Lionello Venturi, *Painting and Painters* (New York: Charles Scribner's Sons, 1945), pp. 152-158.

10. Lionello Venturi, "The Aesthetic Idea of Impressionism," *The Journal of Aesthetics and Art Criticism*, No. 1 (New York: The Philosophical Library, Spring, 1941), p. 34.

11. The German word *Eindruckskunst* for impressionism has many connotations. It seems to be identical with "illusionism" for Werner Weisbach, p. 4, and, as such, is similar to definitions by Ferdinand Brunetière, p. 86, who calls it *don de l'illusion*. The term "impressionism" is applied to "things as they seem to be" by René Huyghe in his most perceptive study "L'impressionnisme et le morcellement de la matière" *Prométhée* (L'Amour de l'Art), Nouvelle Série, No. 1

(Février 1939), pp. 6-16, and by Michel Benamou in the interesting "Symposium on Literary Impressionism," *Yearbook of Comparative and General Literature*, No. 17 (1968), p. 66, etc.

12. R.-M. Albérès applies the term *ultra-impressionnisme* to Nathalie Sarraute's latest creations. including *Les Fruits d'Or* (1953) and *Entre la vie et la mort* (1968). The term *ultra-impressionnisme* has its counterpart in Spanish Literature, often in connection with Miró whose *superimpresionismo* seems to highlight Spanish impressionism with Azorin and Juan Ramón Jiménez. See Benito Varela Jácome, *Renovacion de la novela en el siglo XX* (Barcelona: Ediciones Destino, 1966), p. 136.

There exist nuances of impressionism when Leo Spitzer discusses *transzendentalen*, "transcendental," or *graphischen*, "graphic," impressionism in *Stilstudien*, II, pp. 277, 333; Wylie Sypher's "impressionist realism" in the very disputable study of *Rococo to Cubism in Art and Literature* (New York: Vintage, 1960), p. 181, and Duncan Phillip's "symbolical impressionism" in the very hazy study of *The Enchantment of Art* (New York: John Lane Co., 1914), p. 163.

13. Gustave Geffroy, *La Vie Artistique*, "Salon de 1894" (Paris: E. Dentu, 1895).

14. Leo Spitzer, I, 187.

15. Impressionism is also called *Simultansehen*, "simultaneous vision," or *Farbigwerden der Luft*, "the air that is becoming pure color," by the minor critic Georg Marzynski in "Die impressionistische Methode," *Zeitschrift für Aesthetik und allgemeine Kunstwissenschaft*, XIV (1920), pp. 90, 94. The acknowledged critic Leo Spitzer, in his perceptive article on "Spreizstellung bei präpositionalen Ausdrücken im Französischen (Avec sur la figure grave un bon et doux sourire)," discusses this·phenomenon of simultaneous vision in language referring to Proust. In this respect Proust follows the techniques of the Goncourts, techniques which also occur in impressionistic passages of Pascoli, Deledda and D'Annunzio in Italy; and in Jens Peter Jacobon's *Mogens* (1872) and Herman Bang's *Ved Vejen* (1886) and *Tine* (1889) in Denmark; in Anton Pavlovich Chekhov's *Chayka* (1896), *Tri Sestry* (1901), etc.

16. R.-M. Albérès, *Métamorphoses du roman* (Paris: Albin Michel, 1966), pp. 77-78. ("With them and with their contemporaries an intention appears that we can call 'phenomenological,' and that confirms the vogue of phenomenology among the philosophers and critics after 1940. In this indecisive universe where subjectivism mingles with objectivity, the novel is no longer a story, but a confused colliding of sensations, impressions and experiences. It is not 'ready-made,' shown in advance, shaped and packaged by a trained

writer-narrator. It is suggested to the reader like a fluid, poetic and enigmatic substance, and, instead of following the plot line, we wander around as if in a daydream or as if in life. . . . with Proust, Musil, Kafka, possibly Joyce, and Virginia Woolf (later with Michel Butor and Alain Robbe-Grillet), everything is inverted: *the novel's hero is no longer placed in the world where he lives; rather, the vision of the 'real' world is subject to the relationship between the hero and the world.* . . . the consciousness of the novel's hero dominates the novel and the 'real world' exists only so far as it is reflected by this consciousness.

"In 1890 we would have given this vision of the novel the qualifiation of 'impressionist' or 'subjectivist.' Today we say 'phenomenological.' ")

17.   Pierre-Henri Simon, *Théâtre Destin.* La signification de la renaissance dramatique en France au XXe siècle (Paris: Librairie Armand Colin, 1959), p. 67.

18.   René Huyghe, "L'impressionnisme et la pensée de son temps," *Prométhée* (L'Amour de l'Art), nouvelle série, No. 1 (Février, 1939), p. 9. ("Science and impressionism, each in its own domain, could be summed up by the same formula, the same program: a rational sensualism. . . . Impressionism—a vision of the new universe . . . Science divides matter into billions of atoms which make the universe an immense magma of swirling, infinitesimal particles where the haphazardness and the logic of associations create bodies, shapes, and objects, like so many provisional phantasms. The impressionist for his part practices a similar divisionism: no more contours, no more shapes, no more distinct objects; a powdery haze of colored dots whose convergence and grouping generate an illusion of things. The same profound poetry, the same lyric vision manifests itself here.")

19.   Ruth Moser, *L'Impressionnisme Français: Peinture, littérature, musique* (Geneva: Droz, 1952).

20.   Lionello Venturi, "The Aesthetic Idea of Impressionism," p. 44.

21.   Michel Décaudin, "Poésie impressionniste et poésie symboliste," *Cahiers de l'Association Internationale des Etudes Françaises,* XII (1960), 132-142. ("[impressionism] holds to the real, stablizes the ephemeral; the other [symbolism] is turned toward the absolute, the dream and the ideal.")

22.   Leo Spitzer, *Stilstudien II* (München: Max Hüber Verlag, 1961), p. 296; Helmut Hatzfeld, *Trends and Styles in Twentieth Century French Literature* (Washington: Catholic University of America Press, 1957), p. 210; Oskar Walzel, *Das Wortkunstwerk,*

Mittel seiner Erforschung. "Impressionismus und ästhetische Rubriken," 1914 (Darmstadt: Wissenschaftliche Buchgesellschaft, 1968), pp. 36-44; Elise Richter, "Impresionismo, expresionismo y grammatica" in Charles Bally, Elise Richter, Amado Alonso, and Raimondo Lido, *El Impresionismo en el Lenguage* (Buenos Aires: Universidad de Buenos Aires, 1956), pp. 49-103; Beverly Gibbs, "Impressionism as a Literary Movement."

23. Stephen Ullmann, *Style in the French Novel* (Cambridge: University Press, 1957), p. 142.

24. Leo Spitzer, II, pp. 277, 296, 307.

25. Stephen Ullmann, p. 142.

26. Both stylistic devices are present in Rimbaud's "Fleurs," in *Illuminations*; there are colorful active verbs, *noircissent,* "turn black," *supportant,* "supporting," *entourent,* "surround," and *attirent,* "lure"—elements of expressionist activism. However, the predominant use of nouns either modified by color epithets or themselves evoking a color sensation, e.g., *gradin·d'or,* "a golden step," *les cordons de soie,* "silk cords," *les velours verts,* "green velvets" etc., creates the same intoxication as any of Monet's "Waterlilies," being extremely rich in nuances of color and sensual effects.

27. Helmut Hatzfeld, *Trends and Styles,* p. 210.

28. Concerning impressionism, the only point of agreement among critics is that no Western writer was impressionistic all his life, whereas Japanese writers "by nature tended to be impressionists," Edwin McClellan, "The Impressionist Tendency in some Modern Japanese Writers," *Chicago Review,* XVII, iv (1965), p. 52, and Takéshi Ishikawa, *Etude sur la littérature impressionniste au Japon* (Paris: A Pedone, 1919). It is generally acknowledged that Japanese prints have been a springboard to the impressionist paintings of the late nineteenth century, yet no Western critic seems to acknowledge the fact that Japanese literature offers certainly the oldest literary form of impressionism in their *Zoui-hitsou* or *Man-pitsou.* It should be noted, however, that there is no direct influence of Japanese writers on the Western world.

29. Eugen Lerch, *Handbuch der Frankreichkunde,* 2nd ed. (Frankfurt: Moritz Diesterweg, 1930), Vol. I, pp. 114-118; Werner Weisbach, *Impressionismus, Ein Problem der Malerei in der Antike und Neuzeit* (Berlin: G. Grote'sche Verlagsbuchhandlung, 1919); Richard Hamann, *Der Impressionismus in Leben und Kunst* (Marburg: Kunstgeschichtliches Seminar, 1923), pp. 56-84; Pierre Henri Simon, *Théâtre Destin. La signification de la renaissance dramatique en France au XXe siècle* (Paris: Armand Colin, 1959), p. 67: "L'impressionnisme n'est pas une invention du XXe siècle: c'est une façon

de voir l'homme et le monde, et donc une tendance permanente de l'art." ("Impressionism is not a twentieth century invention: it is a way of seeing man and the world, and therefore a permanent tendency of art."); Maurice Serullaz, *French Painting, The Impressionist Painters*, translated by W. J. Strachan (New York: Universe Books, Inc., 1960), pp. 13-28.

30. Richard Hamann. p. 56.

31. W. Weisbach, *Impressionismus* and Eugen Lerch, *Handbuch der Frankreichkunde*. Examples of this convergence of reality and illusion, we think, find their best indirect expression as early as in the words of Racine's Bérénice: speaking to Phénice (ll. 301-316), she visualizes all the splendor, glory, and power of Titus, mirrored in the many countries he has conquered; all the abstract nouns used in this context are but a reflection and repercussion of her seeing Titus' *rayonnement* in the whole universe; her personal way of seeing Titus transforms itself into a worldview: everything seems to converge to identify Titus with the universe, the personal possessive pronouns, used initially, are replaced by synthetic, neutral pronouns and demonstratives. Melody, harmony, and rhythm of her words are the resonance of her vision of Titus.

32. Michel Décaudin, "Poésie impressionniste et poésie symboliste," in *Cahiers de l'Association Internationale des Etudes Françaises* XII (1960), pp. 132-142.

33. Hamann, *Der Impressionismus in Leben und Kunst.*

34. Helmut A. Hatzfeld, *Literature through Art, A New Approach to French Literature* (New York: Oxford University Press, 1952), p. 165.

35. Walter Melang, "Flaubert als Begründer des literarischen Impressionismus in Frankreich," Dissertation (Emsdetten: Lechte, 1933). He is one of the first critics to reject Brunetière's tendency to base all literary impressionism on painting. See also Helmut Hatzfeld, *Literature through Art*; L. Desprez, *L'évolution naturaliste* (Paris: Tresse, 1884), pp. 94 ff; Eugen Lerch, *Handbuch der Frankreichkunde*; L. Hourticq, "Réalisme et impressionnisme," in *L'Art et la littérature* (Paris: Flammarion, 1946), pp. 217-259.

36. Stephen Ullmann, "New Patterns of Sentence Structure in the Goncourts," *Style in the French Novel* (Cambridge: The University Press, 1957), pp. 121-145.

37. Theodore Robert Bowie, *The Painter in French Fiction, a critical essay* (Chapel Hill: University of North Carolina, 1950); *Studies in the Romance Languages and Literatures*, (1950), No. 15.

38. Rainer Maria Rilke, *Selected Letters 1902-1926*, translated

by R. F. C. Hull (London: Macmillan & Co., Ltd., 1947), October 9, 1907, p. 147.

39.   John Rewald, *Cézanne, sa vie, son oeuvre, son amitié pour Zola* (Paris: Albin Michel, 1939). ("Frenhofer, that's me.")

40.   Emile Zola, *Salons* recueillis, annotés et présentés par F. W. J. Hemmings et Robert J. Niess (Genève: Droz, 1959), pp. 242-243. ("The great misfortune is that not one artist of this group powerfully and definitively realized the formula that they all carried scattered about in their works. The formula is there, divided *ad infinitum*; but nowhere in any of them do we find it applied by a master. They are all precursors, the man of genius is not yet born . . . they remain inferior to the work they attempt, they stammer without being able to find the word. . . . But their influence remains nevertheless enormous, since they are in the only possible evolution; their work contains the future.")

41.   Herbert Howarth, "Symposium on Literary Impressionism," *Yearbook of Comparative and General Literature*, No. 17 (1968), pp. 40-46.

42.   Little known seem to be the impressionist works of the American writer Edgar Saltus (1855-1921), an American aesthete à la Oscar Wilde who wrote such things as *Mary Magdalen* (1892), *Imperial Purple* (1892), and *Purple and Fine Women* (1903). One of the best examples of impressionistic poetry reminding one strongly of the paintings of Renoir and Monet is the poetry of the American Sidney Lanier (1842-1881) with "The Marshes of Glynn" from "Hymns of the Marshes" and John Gould Fletcher's (1886-1950) "Blue Symphony."

43.   R.-M. Albérès, "Aux sources du nouveau roman: L'impressionnisme anglais," *Revue de Paris*, LXIX (May, 1962), pp. 74-86. ("With the appearance of Henry James and Joseph Conrad, the art of Nathalie Sarraute, Michel Butor and even Alain Robbe-Grillet is born.")

44.   R. M. Albérès, "Plongées dans les Profondeurs de l'Impressionnisme" in *Histoire du Roman Moderne* (Paris, 1962), pp. 181-198: "De Virginia Woolf à Nathalie Sarraute tout un art existe, qui cherche à saisir le jaillissement premier de l'impression, le 'courant de conscience,' et il n'est que trop aisé d'évoquer à ce sujet l'ombre de Bergson." ("From Virginia Woolf to Nathalie Sarraute quite an art exists that tries to seize the first bursting forth of an impression, the 'stream of consciousness,' and, considering this, it is only too easy to evoke a reflection of Bergson.") See also R.-M. Albérès, "Le présent et l'éternel," in *L'Aventure Intellectuelle du XXe Siècle* (Paris, 1959), pp. 159-163.

45. Pierre Francastel, *Peinture et Société* (Paris: NRF Gallimard, 1965), p. 126: "Loin de voir dans l'impressionnisme un 'mouvement' de courte durée, j'y vois donc le point de départ d'une enquête qui, à travers les jeux capricieux de la mode et les compromis nécessaires avec la tradition, se poursuit encore sous nos yeux." ("Far from viewing impressionism as a short-lived 'movement,' I see it as the starting point of an inquiry that, even through the capricious games of fashion and the compromises necessary with tradition, is still being pursued under our very eyes.")

46. Pierre Francastel, "La Fin de l'Impressionnisme: Esthétique et Causalité," in *Problems of the 19th and 20 Century Studies in Western Art*, Acts of the 20th International Congress of the History of Art, IV (Princeton, 1963), p. 128. ("It is thus evident that the circumstances and the causes of the evolution which set in about 1885 cannot result in a determination of the manner in which impressionism gave way to other movements of equal consequence for the history of art and culture. Consequently, it is impossible to define the moment, the circumstances and the causes of the decline of a movement which has become a standard pattern for the spirit.")

Chapter Two

1. Marcel Proust, *Le Temps Retrouvé* (Paris: Le Livre de Poche, 1954), p. 237. ("Only the impression, however trivial its material may seem to be, however faint its traces, is a criterion of truth and deserves for that reason to be apprehended by the mind, for the mind. . . .")

2. Proust, *Le Temps Retrouvé*, p. 240. ("The reality that he has to express resides, as I now began to understand, not in the superficial appearance of his subject but at a depth at which that appearance matters little; this truth had been symbolized for me by that chink of a spoon against a plate, that starched stiffness of a napkin, which had been of more value to me for my spiritual renewal than innumerable conversations of a humanitarian or patriotic or internationalistic or metaphysical kind.")

3. Proust, *Le Temps Retrouvé*, p. 255. ("How could the literature of description possibly have any value, when it is only beneath the surface of the little things which such a literature describes that reality has its hidden existence (grandeur, for example, in the distant sound of an aeroplane or the outline of the steeple of Saint-Hilaire, the past in the taste of a madeleine, and so on) and when the things in themselves are without significance until it has been extracted from them?")

4. Lionello Venturi, *Painting and Painters,* How to look at a pic-

ture, from Giotto to Chagall (New York: Charles Scribner's Sons, 1945), p. 152.

5. Joseph Conrad, *The Nigger of the "Narcissus,"* (London: J. M. Dent and Sons Ltd., 1897), Preface, p. ix.

6. Maurice Merleau-Ponty, "The Problem of Speech," *Themes from the Lectures at the College de France 1952-1960,* translated by John O'Neill (Evanston: Northwestern University Press, 1970), p. 25.

7. Wylie Sypher, *Rococo to Cubism in Art and Literature* (New York: A Vintage Book, 1960), p. 171.

8. Hugo Sommerhalder, *Zum Begriff des literarischen Impressionismus* (Zürich: Poligraphischer Verlag, 1961), p. 16. ("If we are in such a mood that inner and outer worlds coincide, then the conditions are fulfilled for the assimilation of the ego and the impressions from the outside world—and for the fusion of outer and inner space into one single space. The mood is the medium in which impressionistic literature condenses itself.")

9. Maurice Merleau-Ponty, *Sens et Non-Sens* (Paris: Editions Nagel, 1948), p. 24. ("He does not put the dividing line between 'the senses' and 'intelligence,' but between the spontaneous order of objects perceived and the human order of ideas and science.")

10. Proust, *Le Temps Retrouvé,* p. 237. ("The impression is for the writer what experiment is for the scientist, with the difference that in the scientist the work of intelligence precedes the experiment and in the writer it comes after the impression.")

11. *The Nigger of the "Narcissus,"* p. x.

12. Jules Laforgue, *Mélanges Posthumes,* "Critique d'art," "L'impressionnisme" (Paris: Mercure de France, 1903), pp. 137, 144. ("The impressionist sees and represents nature just as it is, that is, solely in colored vibrations. Not design, nor light, nor relief, nor perspective, nor chiaroscuro—such childish classifications: in reality all of that is resolved in colored vibrations and must be obtained on the canvas solely through colored vibrations. . . . The object and the subject are then irretrievably moving, unseizable and unseizing.")

13. André Gide, *Les Nourritures Terrestres* (Paris: Le Livre de Poche, 1917-36). ("I do not wish to teach you any other wisdom but life!")

14. R.-M. Albérès, *Histoire de roman moderne,* "Plongées dans les profondeurs de l'Impressionnisme" (Paris: Albin Michel, 1962), p. 186. ("Multiple, swirling around, made of luminous dust suspended in nothingness, impressionist reality is not *told,* nor is it even *described* at all. Words and men's meager gestures, their hesitations and arabesques, scarcely indicate several lines on the surface of that nebula of reality that is 'Life.' Bewildered by a new perspective, the

reader is thus transported into a molten universe. . . . Far from being an objective vision, impressionism is in effect a plunge into the consciousness.")

15. Pierre Decaves, "Réalités du roman," *La Table Ronde*, No. 157 (Janvier, 1961), p. 165. ("I was haunted by two things: discontinuity, the fragmentary aspect of the emotions that we feel and that are never tied to each other, and at the same time their contiguity in the consciousness. My sentence tries to translate this contiguity. The use of the present participle allows me to put myself outside conventional time. When we say: he went to such and such a place, we give the impression of an act that has a beginning and an end. Well, there is neither beginning nor end to a memory.")

16. Emile Zola, *Salons*, recueillis, annotés et présentés par F. W. J. Hemmings, et Robert J. Niess (Genève: Droz, 1959), p. 194. ("Their discovery [of the impressionists] properly consists of having recognized that intense light fades colors that the sun reflected by objects tends, by sheer brightness, to bring them to this luminous unity that blends its seven prismatic colors into a single tone of dim brilliance, of light. Colors dissolve into light in the brilliant clarity of full sunshine.")

17. Zola, *Salons*, pp. 240-241. ("This study of light in its thousands of decompositions and recompositions is what we called, more or less accurately, impressionism, because from then on, a painting becomes the impression of a moment experienced in the presence of nature.")

18. Gustave Flaubert, *L'Education Sentimentale* (Paris: Garnier Frères, 1964), p. 9. ("the luminous point towards which all things converged.")

19. Flaubert, *L'Education Sentimentale*, p. 50. See also, pp. 209, 290. ("The streets were deserted. Now and then a heavy wagon would roll past, shaking the pavements. The houses came one after another with their grey fronts, their closed windows; and he thought with disdain of all those human beings who lived behind those walls without having seen her, and not one of whom dreamed of her existence. He had no consciousness of his surroundings, of space, of anything, and striking the ground with the heel, rapping with his walking-stick on the shutters of the shops, he kept walking on continually at random, in a state of excitement, carried away by his emotions. Suddenly he felt himself surrounded by a circle of damp air, and found that he was on the edge of the quays.")

20. Charles Baudelaire, *Oeuvres Complètes* (Paris: Pleïade, Gallimard, 1954), p. 679: "La vie parisienne est féconde en sujets poétiques et merveilleux. Le merveilleux nous enveloppe et nous abreuve comme

l'atmosphère, mais nous ne le voyons pas." ("Parisian life profuses wonderfully poetic subjects. Their marvel envelops and drenches us like the atmosphere, but we don't see it.")

21. *L'Education Sentimentale*, pp. 65-66. ("Occasionally he was attracted towards the boulevards by the hope of finding there something that might amuse him. After he had passed through dark alleys, from which his nostrils were greeted by fresh moist odours, he reached vast, desolate, open spaces, dazzling with light, in which monuments cast at the side of the pavements notches of black shadow. But once more the wagons and the shops appeared, and the crowd had the effect of stunning him, especially on Sunday, when, from the Bastille to the Madeleine, it kept swaying in one immense flood over the asphalt, in the midst of a cloud of dust, in an incessant clamour. He felt disgusted at the meanness of the faces, the silliness of the talk, and the idiotic self-satisfaction that oozed through these sweating foreheads. However, the consciousness of being superior to these individuals mitigated the weariness which he experienced in gazing at them.")

22. André Gide, *Les Nourritures Terrestres* (Paris: Le Livre de Poche, Gallimard, 1917-36), p. 121. ("I learned to judge all creatures by their receptivity of light; . . .")

23. *Ibid.*, p. 28.

24. *Ibid.*, p. 132. ("Have you noticed that in this book there is *no one*? And even I myself am nothing in it but Vision. . . . Till the night was drawn to an end I clung to the hope of a new light.")

25. *Ibid.*, p. 139. ("You cannot imagine, Nathaniel, the effect produced by this saturation of light, and the sensual ecstasy that comes from this persistent heat. . . . An olive branch in the sky; the sky above the hills; the song of a flute at a café door. . . . Algiers was so hot, so full of rejoicings, that I determined to leave it for two or three days; but at Blida, where I took refuge, I found the orange trees in flower. . . .

I go out as soon as it is morning; I walk; I look at nothing and see everything; a marvelous symphony of subconscious sensations is formed and harmonized within me. Time passes; my excitement abates, like the sun's course, which becomes slower as it becomes more vertical. Then I choose something—a creature or a thing—to fall in love with; but it must be something moving, for directly my emotion becomes fixed, it ceases to be vital. I feel then, at every fresh moment that I have never before seen, never before tasted anything. I follow madly in a wild pursuit the things that fly and escape me. Yesterday I ran up to the top of the hills that look down upon Blida, in order to keep the sun in sight a moment longer; in order to see the sun set and the clouds shed their glow on to the white terraces. I surprise shade and silence under the trees; I roam furtively in the light of the moon; I often have the sensation of swimming, the warm luminous air enwraps and uplifts me so gently.")

26. André Gide, *Les Faux Monnayeurs* (Paris: Le Livre de Poche, Gallimard, 1925), p. 230. ("The novel has never known that 'formidable erosion of contours,' as Nietzsche calls it; . . .")

27. John Rewald, *The History of Impressionism* (New York: The Museum of Modern Art, 1961), p. 578. Cézanne told a German collector: "I try to render perspective solely by the means of color; the main thing in a picture is to achieve distance. By that one recognizes a painter's talent."

28. Jean Hytier, *André Gide* (Garden City, N.Y.: Doubleday & Co., 1962), p. 62.

29. Charles Baudelaire, *Oeuvres Complètes*, p. 614. ("Harmony is the basis of the theory of color. Melody is the unity of color, or general color. Melody needs a conclusion; it is a whole where all effects combine for a general effect.")

30. Hermann Bahr, *Zur Überwindung des Naturalismus*. Theoretische Schriften 1887-1904 (Stuttgart, Berlin, Köln, Mainz: Kohlhammer Verlag, 1968), pp. 197-198. ("All distinctions are here eliminated, the physical and the psychological coincide, and sensations are one and the same, the ego dissolves and everything is an eternal flux which in some places seems to stop, in others to flow swifter, everything is merely a movement of colors, sounds, temperatures, pressures, spaces and times, which on this side of the ego appears as moods, feelings, and desires. . . . before long Mach's world view will probably be called simply 'philosophy of impressionism.'")

31. Pierre Francastel, *Peinture et Société* (Paris: NRF Gallimard, 1965), p. 123. Francastel, in 1951, conceives as a major problem the question of the real influence the recording of light had on the manner of representing space: "Le vrai problème consiste à savoir quelle influence réelle l'enregistrement des sensations lumineuses a eu sur le mode de représentation de l'espace." ("The real problem lies in knowing what actual influence the recording of light sensations has had on the method of representing space.")

Chapter Three

1. Leo Spitzer, *Stilstudien* I (München: Max Hüber Verlag, 1961), pp. 4-6. Spitzer explains the impressionist's use of the diary as being an evolution of stage directions, such as, dix heures du soir, la nuit, un grand bruit de ferraille. Later a kind of *style sténographique* was used

in official German, and also by businessmen on posters. Besides this evolution there is a literary trend: the realistic observation contributed to the rendering of instantaneous sketches.

2.   Ortega y Gasset, *The Dehumanization of Art and other Writings on Art and Literature* (Garden City, N.Y.: Doubleday, 1956), pp. 50-51.

3.   Charles Baudelaire, "Salon de 1845" in *Oeuvres Complètes* (Paris: Pleïade, 1954), p. 586. (". . . there is a great difference between a piece that is created and a piece that is finite . . . in general, what is created is not finite, and . . . a very finite thing cannot be created at all. . . .")

4.   André Gide, *Les Nourritures Terrestres* (Paris: Le Livre de Poche, 1917-36), p. 52. ("Vincigliata. It was there I first saw clouds dissolving in the blue sky; it astonished me greatly, for I had no idea they could melt into the azure in this way, and had always thought they went on getting heavier and heavier until they turned into rain. But no; I watched them disappearing, cloudlet after cloudlet, until nothing was left but the azure. It was a marvelous death—a vanishing in the midst of heaven.")

5.   André Gide, *Les Faux-Monnayeurs* (Paris: Le Livre de Poche, 1925), p. 231.

6.   Roger Martin du Gard, *Recollections of André Gide* (New York: The Viking Press, 1953), pp. 27-28.

7.   Jean Mouton, "L'Optique de Proust, du regard à la vision," *Entretiens sur Marcel Proust* sous la direction de Georges Cattaui et Philip Kolb (Paris, La Haye: Mouton & Co., 1966), pp. 50-51. M. Poulet asks in this connection a very pertinent question: ". . . s'agit-il de la sensation elle-même et dans cette hypothèse, faut-il voir dans Proust et les impressionnistes . . . des êtres pour qui la sensation dans sa nudité importe avant tout, ou bien, placés dans la perspective des interprétations de Sartre ou de Merleau-Ponty, nous trouvons-nous en présence d'une transformation pour ainsi dire spontanée de la sensation par lar perception, étant entendu que la perception coïncide avec une création progressive du sujet regardant?" (". . . is it a question of the sensation itself and, following this hypothesis, must we see in Proust and the impressionists . . . beings for whom pure sensation is all important, or indeed, placed within the perspective of the interpretations of Sartre or Merleau-Ponty, are we present at a spontaneous transformation (so to speak) of the sensation by perception, on the understanding that perception coincides with the progressive creation by the onlooker?")

8.   Marcel Proust, *Le Temps Retrouvé* (Paris: Le Livre de Poche, 1954), p. 249. ("An hour is not merely an hour, it is a vase full of

scents and sounds and projects and climates, and what we call reality is a certain connection between these immediate sensations and the memories which envelop us simultaneously with them . . . truth will be attained by him only when he takes two different objects, states the connection between them—a connection analogous in the world of art to the unique connection which in the world of science is provided by the law of causality—and encloses them in the necessary links of a well-wrought style; truth—and life too—can be attained by us only when, by comparing a quality common to two sensations, we succeed in extracting their common essence and in reuniting them to each other, liberated from the contingencies of time, within a metaphor.")

9. Alain Robbe-Grillet. *Pour le Nouveau Roman* (Paris: NRF Gallimard, 1963), p. 150. ("Why seek to re-create clock time in a story concerned only with human time? Isn't it wiser to think about our own memory which is never chronological?")

10. *The Journals of André Gide*, Vol. I, 1889-1913, translated by Justin O'Brien (New York: Alfred A. Knopf, 1947), pp. 29-30.

11. Hermann Bahr, *Expressionismus* (München: Delphin Verlag, 1918), pp. 38-39. ("Perception is simultaneously experience and reaction.") "Wie der Mensch zur Welt steht, so sieht er sie. . . . Sehen ist zugleich ein Leiden und ein Handeln des Menschen. Je nachdem er sich dabei mehr leidend oder mehr handelnd verhält, passiv oder aktiv, je nachdem er entweder möglichst rein empfangen oder es möglichst stark erwidern will, verändert sich das Sehen, verändert sich das Bild. Immer besteht Sehen aus zwei Tätigkeiten, einer äusseren und einer inneren, einer, die dem Menschen angetan wird, und einer, die dann der Mensch ihr antut." ("As man stands in relationship to the world so does he perceive it. . . . Perception is simultaneously experience and reaction. Depending on whether he relates in a more experiencing or reacting manner, i.e., passively or actively, and depending on whether he wishes to be a pure receptor or to react rather strongly, perception and image change. This perception always consists of two acts, an outer and an inner one, one, which man undergoes, and the other, which man opposes to the first one.")

12. Charles Baudelaire, *Oeuvres Complètes, Les Fleurs du Mal,* "Les Bijoux" (Paris: Pleïade, 1957). ("furiously things thoughtless where the sound with color mixes";) It was Baudelaire, who in his 1840 Salon, called England "the fatherland of exasperate colourists." Was he thinking of Turner, who was so well acquainted with Goethe's *Farbenlehre?* We should also remember the influence of Delacroix as a colorist on impressionist writers and painters. To Delacroix, color is one of the chief means by which a painter endows his work with the semblance of life. Acquainted with the work of Chevreul on *De la Loi*

du Contraste Simultanée des Couleurs (1829) he records observations on the color of shadows in his journal. Paul Signac's *D'Eugène Delacroix au Néo-Impressionnisme* explains Delacroix's persistent influence on the impressionist painters. Cézanne is reported to have said speaking for himself and his famous contemporaries: "We are all in Delacroix!" Monet, Renoir, Seurat, Gauguin, Van Gogh, they all were inspired by Delacroix' use of color.

13. Hugo Sommerhalder. *Zum Begriff des literarischen Impressionismus* (Zürich: Poligraphischer Verlag, 1961), p. 11. ("The impressionist has neither temporal nor historical roots which could stabilize the human being.")

14. André Gide, *Les Nourritures Terrestres* (Paris: Le Livre de Poche, 1917-36), p. 136. ("suffocation; risings; fallings.–Helplessness; what am I? A cork–a wretched cork on the waters. Oh, to abandon oneself to the oblivion of the waves; to enjoy the luxury of renouncement; to become a thing.")

15. André Gide, *The Journals,* translated by Justin O'Brien, Vol. III: 1928-39 (New York: Alfred A. Knopf, 1949), June 12, 1931.

16. As early as with Jongkind there are no people at all. Later, Manet, in "Luncheon in the Studio," organizes the entire composition about the silhouette of a young man. Around him, various forms of still-life are arranged in a mysterious and poetic interplay. The charm of the work lies in the relationships of tones and forms. The closed face of the young man seems to be without a soul. Monet, in "The River," presents a feminine silhouette that marks the foreground. It is not anecdotal: because of the light colors that she brings to this area, she serves solely as a juncture between the shaded and the light areas.

17. R.-M. Albérès, *Histoire du Roman Moderne* (Paris: Albin Michel, 1962), p. 190. ("For the new sensitivity, life is a murky profundity where the light of consciousness scintillates, diffracts and dissolves before disappearing, like the rays of the sun which are slowly diffused, then absorbed into the water up to the blackness of its depths.")

18. Gustave Flaubert, *L'Education Sentimentale* (Paris: Garnier Frères, 1964), p. 414. ("It was as if portions of his heart had been carried away with these things; and the monotony of the same voices and the same gestures benumbed him with fatigue, and caused within him a mournful torpor, a sensation like that of death itself.")

19. Jean Pierre Richard, *Littérature et Sensation* (Paris: Editions du Seuil, 1954), p. 148, quotes Gustave Flaubert, *Correspondance I,* p. 287. ("I do not even believe in myself, I do not know if I am silly or bright, good or bad, miserly or extravagant. Like everyone else, *I am floating between all that.* My merit probably is in having realized

this, and my shortcoming in having the frankness to say so. Moreover, are we sure of our Selves? Are we sure of what we think, of what we feel?")

20. Rainer Maria Rilke, *Sämtliche Werke, Sechster Band,* "Die Aufzeichnungen des Malte Laurids Brigge" (Frankfurt am Main: Inselverlag, 1966), p. 712. ("Other people put their faces on, one after the other, with uncanny rapidity and wear them out. At first it seems to them they are provided for always; but they scarcely reach forty—and they have come to the last. This naturally has something tragic. They are not accustomed to taking care of faces, their last is worn through in a week, has holes, and in many places is thin as paper; and then little by little the under layer, the no-face, comes through, and they go about with that.")

21. Leo Spitzer, *Stilstudien I* (München: Max Hüber Verlag, 1961), p. 207, quotes Barrès, *Leurs Figures,* p. 768. ("Certain Germans do not say 'I think' but 'something is thinking in myself'; we are profoundly affective beings.") Spitzer also quotes passages in Péguy, Claudel, Duhamel.

22. Rimbaud, *Oeuvres* (Paris: Garnier, 1960), "A Georges Izambard," "A Paul Demeny à Douai," 13 mai 1871 and 15 mai 1871, p. 345. ("It is wrong to say I think. One should say: I am thought. . . . For I is someone else. . . . To me this is evident: I witness the birth of my thought. I look at it, I listen to it: I give a stroke of the bow: the symphony begins to stir in the depth or comes bursting unto stage.")

23. Jean-Paul Sartre, *La Nausée* (Paris: Le Livre de Poche, 1938), pp. 142-143. ("My thought is *me*: that's why I can't stop. I exist because I think . . . and I can't stop myself from thinking.")

24. Jean-Paul Sartre, *La Mort dans l'Ame* (Paris: Le Livre de Poche, 1949), p. 125. ("We are a verminous dream, our thoughts thicken, become less and less human; hairy, clawed thoughts that scurry around from head to head; the vermin kingdom is about to inherit the earth.")

25. Sartre, *La Mort dans l'Ame,* p. 84. ("Why do you say *they* did everything they could? If you felt like a Frenchman, you'd have said *we.*")

26. Stéphane Mallarmé, *Correspondance 1862-1871,* éd. Henri Mondor (Paris: NRF Gallimard, 1959), p. 242, "Letter to Cazalis." ("I have just spent a frightening year: my Thought has thought itself through and has arrived at a Divine Concept. . . . This is to tell you that I am now impersonal and no longer the Stéphane you knew — but an aptitude of the spiritual universe for seeing and developing itself through what I was.")

27. *Les Nourritures Terrestres,* p. 155.

28. *Ibid.*, p. 58. ("my body seemed at times to have no limits; it was prolonged outside myself, or sometimes became porous; I felt myself deliciously melting away, like sugar.")

29. Rainer Maria Rilke, *Sämtliche Werke*, Sechster Band, "Die Aufzeichnungen des Malte Laurids Brigge" (Frankfurt am Main: Inselverlag, 1966), p. 808. ("I lost all sense, I simply ceased to exist. For one second I had an indescribable, painful and futile longing for myself, then there was only he: there was nothing but he.")

30. *Ibid.*, pp. 768-774.

Chapter Four

1. Some critics consider Verlaine's *Art Poétique* as the impressionist poets' manifesto, and the *Journal* of the Goncourts as the manifesto of impressionist prose. Both works are major contributions to impressionism, but do not contain all the devices used by impressionist authors.

2. Camille Mauclair, *Monet* (New York: Dodd, Mead, and Co., 1924), p. 27.

3. R.-M. Albérès presents the view that the modern French novel is an outgrowth of the Baudelairian prose poem in *L'Aventure Intellectuelle du XXe siècle* and *Histoire du Roman Moderne,* and on a larger scale, Remy de Gourmont in *Couleurs* (Paris: Mercure de France, 1920), confirms as much: ". . . un roman est un poème et doit être conçu et exécuté comme tel, pour être valable. . . . Le roman ne relève pas d'une autre esthétique que le poème; le roman originel fut en vers." ("A novel is a poem and must be conceived and realized as such in order to be appreciated. . . . The novel does not spring from any other aesthetics but the poem; the first novel was written in verse.")

4. Edgar Allan Poe, *Literary Criticism of Edgar Poe*, ed. Robert L. Hough (Lincoln: University of Nebraska Press, 1965), p. 40.

5. Honoré de Balzac, *Le Lys dans la Vallée* (Paris: Garnier Frères, 1966), pp. 115-119. ("it struck me that there was a harmony in their hues and foliage, a poetry that found its way to the understanding by fascinating the eye, just as musical phrases arouse a thousand associations in loved and loving hearts. If color has organic light, must it not have its meaning, as vibrations of the air have? Helped by Jacques and Madeleine, . . . I set to work to compose two nosegays by which I intended to symbolize a sentiment. . . . Or a long forest avenue, like the nave of a cathedral where the pillars are trees, their branches meeting like the groins of a vault, and at the end a distant glade seen through the foliage, dappled with light and shade, or glowing in the

ruddy beams of sunset like the painted glass window of a choir, filled with birds for choristers. . . . And over these pictures cast floods of sunshine, rippling like a nourishing tide, or piles of gray cloud in bars like the furrows on an old man's brow, or the cool tones of a faintly yellow sky banded with pale light—and listen! You will hear vague harmonies in the depth of bewildering silence. 'Dear! how lovely that is!' You can imagine this enchanting communication through the arrangement of a nosegay, . . .")

6. *Literary Criticism of Edgar Poe*, pp. 31-32.

7. Jean Pierre Richard, *Littérature et Sensation* (Paris: Editions du Seuil, 1954), p. 148.

8. Pierre Henri Simon, *Théâtre Destin*, La signification de la renaissance dramatique en France au XXe siècle (Paris: Armand Colin, 1959,), p. 72. (*"But there are no plots, only themes."*)

9. Jean Rousset, "Madame Bovary or the Book about Nothing," in *Flaubert*, a collection of critical essays, ed. by Raymond Giraud (Englewood Cliffs, N.J.: Prentice-Hall, 1964), p. 113, quotes Flaubert, *Correspondance II*, p. 345.

10. Marcel Proust, *Oeuvres Complètes*, X. *Chroniques* "A propos du style de Flaubert" (Paris: Gallimard, 1927), p. 196. ("Things have as much life as men, because reasoning assigns external causes to all visual phenomena, but this cause is not implied in the first impression we receive.")

11. Proust, *Chroniques*, "A propos du style de Flaubert," p. 198. ("whose protagonists generally are things . . . , who in this continued vision are no more than things, but no less.")

12. *Ibid.*, p. 196. (". . . in *L'Education Sentimentale*, the revolution has been accomplished; what until Flaubert had been action, becomes impression.")

13. André Gide, *Les Nourritures Terrestres* (Paris: Le Livre de Poche, 1917-36), p. 132. ("I see a generation coming up and I see a generation going down. I see a vast generation coming up, coming up to life, all armed, all armed with joy.")

14. *Ibid.*, p. 92. ("The moon showed between the branches of the ilex trees, monotonous, but lovely as ever. They were talking now in groups and I heard only a sentence here and there; everyone seemed to be speaking to everyone else of love, without heeding that no one listened.

"Then, as the moon disappeared behind the darkened branches of the ilex trees, the conversation died away, and they lay quiet beside one another among the leaves, vaguely listening to the one or two voices that still lingered on, but more and more softly, till soon they only reached us mingled with the murmur of the stream in its mossy bed.")

15. André Gide, *Les Cahiers et les Poésies d'André Walter* (Paris: NRF Gallimard, 1952), p. 97. ("Should I write in French? No, I would like to write in the language of music.")

16. Marcel Proust, *Oeuvres Complètes*, IX, *Les Plaisirs et les Jours* (Paris: NRF Gallimard, 1935) pp. 188-189. ("All at once, a slight swishing arose slowly and restlessly, swiftly grew and seemed to roll across the woods. It was the shiver of leaves crumpled by the breeze. One by one I heard them breaking like the waves upon the vast silence of complete night. Then this same sound faded and died away. In the narrow meadow strung out before me between two thick rows of oaks, a river of light seemed to flow, contained by these two shadow-wharves. The moonlight, although evoking the keeper's house, the leafy branches and a sailing boat out of the nothingness of night, had not awakened them. In sleep's silence, the moon had lighted up only the vague phantom of their shape without having been able to distinguish the contours that made them so real to me during the day and that oppressed me by their certain presence and perpetual banal proximity. The doorless house, the stemless, almost leafless foliage, and the boatless sail seemed, instead of a cruelly undeniable and monotonously habitual reality, to be a strange, inconsistent and luminous dream of slumbering trees plunging into obscurity. . . . The only reality was this unreal light and I evoked it with a smile. I did not understand what mysterious similarity was uniting my cares with the solemn mysteries being celebrated in the woods, in heaven and on the sea; I sensed that their explanation, their solace and their pardon had been proffered and that it was unimportant that my intelligence was not in on the secret, since my heart understood it so well.")

17. "Claude Simon, franc-tireur de la révolution romanesque," an interview by Thérèse de Saint-Phalle in *Le Figaro Littéraire* (April 6, 1967). ("When I began to write I had no ideas to communicate. . . . at the start, I tried to find verbal equivalents of vague feelings. . . . From the moment we no longer undertake to communicate ideas that existed before writing, things appear quite different. If I wrote: 'He stamped the letter,' that's abstract. If, on the contrary, I speak of a green stamp and the taste of the glue on the tongue that licks it, etc., writing immediately becomes 'sensorial,' and, as it were, 'concrete.' . . . An incessant story such as we describe in the traditional novel, is artificially reconstructed; it is neither perceived nor felt.")

18. Claude Simon, *L'Herbe* (Paris: Editions de Minuit, 1958), p. 9. ("But she has nothing, nobody, and no one will mourn for her (and what's death without tears?) except maybe her brother, and he's

an old man now, and probably no more than she would mourn herself, I mean would allow herself to mourn herself, decide it was decent, was suitable to. . . .")

19. R.-M. Albérès, *Le roman d'aujourd'hui 1960-1970* (Paris: Albin Michel, 1970), p. 217. ("This is possibly the book's subject: a writer busy playing with words in the middle of the confused din of men.")

20. Maurice Merleau-Ponty, "The Problem of Speech," *Themes from the Lectures at the Collège de France 1952-60*, translated by John O'Neill (Evanston: Northwestern University Press, 1970), p. 25.

21. Jean-Paul Sartre, *La Nausée* (Paris: Le Livre de Poche, 1937), p. 7.

22. James Joyce, *The Portable James Joyce* (New York: The Viking Press, 1958), p. 396.

23. Brunetière, Proust, Brombert, Lerch, Melang, and Wellek have done intensive studies on Flaubert's use of the imperfect. The most significant study is the one of Proust who was the first to discover the new use of the imperfect in Flaubert. In "A Propos du Style de Flaubert," *Chroniques*, pp. 197-199: "Le subjectivisme de Flaubert s'exprime par un emploi nouveau des temps des verbes, des prépositions, des adverbes, les deux derniers n'ayant presque jamais dans sa phrase qu'une valeur rythmique. Un état qui se prolonge est indiqué par l'imparfait. . . . donc cet imparfait, si nouveau dans la littérature, change entièrement l'aspect des choses et des êtres. . . . Cet imparfait sert à rapporter non seulement les paroles mais toute la vie des gens. *L'Education Sentimentale* est un long rapport de toute une vie, sans que les personnages prennent pour ainsi dire une part active à l'action. Parfois le parfait interrompt l'imparfait, mais devient alors comme lui quelque chose d'infini qui se prolonge. . . ." ("Flaubert's subjectivism is expressed by a new use of verb tenses, prepositions, and adverbs, the last two almost never having but a rhythmic value within the sentence. A prolonged state is indicated by the imperfect. . . . then this imperfect, so new in literature, completely changes the aspect of things and of beings. . . . This imperfect serves to relate not only the words, but an entire life without its characters' taking an active part, so to speak, in the action. Sometimes the perfect interrupts the imperfect, but then becomes, like it, something infinite that is prolonged. . . .")

24. Gustave Flaubert, *L'Education Sentimentale* (Paris: Garnier, 1964), pp. 2, 4. ("The hubbub had subsided. The passengers had all taken their places. Some of them stood warming themselves around the machinery, and the chimney spat forth with a slow, rhythmic rattle its plume of black smoke. Little drops of dew trickled over the

copper plates; the deck quivered with the vibration from within; and the two paddle-wheels, rapidly turning round, lashed the water. . . . The surrounding country at this point had an empty look. In the sky there were little white clouds which remained motionless, and the sense of weariness, which vaguely diffused itself over everything, seemed to retard the progress of the steamboat and to add to the insignificant appearance of the passengers.")

25. Jean-Paul Sartre, *La Mort dans l'Ame* (Paris: Le Livre de Poche, Gallimard, 1949), p. 113. ("The procession had vanished. As far as eye could reach, silence and emptiness, an abyss stretching horizontally away from him. He felt tired; the streets led nowhere; without human life, they all looked alike. The boulevard Saint-Michel, but yesterday a long southward spread of gold, seemed now like a stranded whale, belly upwards.")

26. *Ibid.*, pp. 341-343. ("The face vanished and the dream began. The shadows of the bars crept slowly across the floor, slipped, bending, over the prostrate bodies, scaled the crates, bent and bent again, and then grew dim; darkness scaled the walls. Through the bars the skylight looked like a bruise, a pallid bruise, a black bruise, which turned suddenly to a bright and mocking eye. The bars resumed their progress, turning and turning around; the darkness turned like the lamp of a lighthouse; the beast was in its cage. For a moment men scurried, then disappeared. The ship drifted from the shore with all the convicts dead from hunger in their cages. A match sputtered; on one of the crates a label in red letters said, at an angle: FRAGILE. . . . Fragile. What is fragile? We are all fragile. The savor, on the tongue, twists, turns like a solar whirlpool, an ancient taste, forgotten, I have forgotten, *the sun swarming in the leaves of the chestnut trees, a shower of sunlight upon my forehead, I was in the hammock reading, the white house behind me, behind me Touraine, I loved the trees, the sun, and the house, I loved the world and happiness, oh, long ago.* . . . He fell back into sticky sap, into SUBJECTIVITY. . . .")

27. Without claiming a direct affinity between some of Monet's scenes of the "Seine à Vétheuil," "Le Givre," or "Vétheuil, soleil couchant," and Antonioni's film, there seems to be the same basic conception of merging water and sky, land and sea into an atmospheric "impression" conveying the deep melancholy in which the protagonists are caught up.

28. *The Dehumanization of Art*, p. 112.

29. Compare with their work Monet's "Londres, le Parlement trouée de soleil dans le brouillard," "Vétheuil, soleil couchant," "La Seine à Port-Villez," "La Seine à Vétheuil," "Impression, Mist," etc.,

and Pissarro's "Ile Lacroix, Rouen–Effect of Fog," etc., as mentioned above.

30. Maurice Serullaz, *French Painting, The Impressionist Painters,* translated by W. J. Strachan (New York: 1960), p. 16. Serullaz recognizes the literary and painterly inspiration of Debussy, in reference to all the creations whose themes are most popular with all impressionists: "All through his [Debussy's] career the titles of his compositions suggest things that Claude Monet and his friends were eager to express in paint: *The Fountain* (after Baudelaire, 1890), *Clouds* (Nocturnes, 1898), *Sketches, Gardens in the Rain* (Estampes, 1903), *The Sea,* (*From Dawn to Noon on the Sea, Waves at Play, Dialogue between the Wind and the Sea.* 1905), *Reflections in the Water* (Images, 1905-1907), *Steps on the Snow, What the West Wind Saw, Sails, The Wind over the Plain, Sounds and Perfumes rise in the Evening Air* (after Baudelaire), *The Submerged Cathedral* (Préludes, Book No. 1, 1910), *Mists, Dead Leaves, Heath, Ondine, Fireworks* (Préludes, Book No. 2, 1913), etc."

31. This erosion of contours we find also in Monet's "Reflets Verts," "Soleil Couchant," "Londres, le Parlement troué de soleil dans le brouillard," in Manet's and in Renoir's boating scenes on the Seine, to mention just a few.

32. The most perceptive study on Verlaine's impressionism is Octave Nadal's book on *Paul Verlaine* (Paris: Mercure de France, 1941).

33. Anna Balakian in her recent study on the *Symbolist Movement* (New York: Random House, 1967), pp. 37-39, calls it "one of the genuine models of symbolist poetry," and then turns to the "Romantic ingredients" which indeed are not romantic at all, yet the very essence of impressionism: "First, there is no direct statement of the poet's emotions: whatever we sense of the condition of his feelings comes to us through the indirect discourse of the imagery. Second, there is no transcendentalism: the memory which is evoked through the perfume is contained within its physical confines of the perfume itself; there is no parallelism between the physical state and an ideal or heavenly vision, only the sun drowning in its own blood as a projection of the sinking of the poet's heart into its own abyss."

34. Jules Laforgue, *Oeuvres Complètes, Mélanges Posthumes,* "L'Art Impressionniste" (Paris: Mercure de France, 1903), pp. 176-77. Laforgue defines what he means by "ligne brisée": "L'idéal est la ligne mille fois brisée, pétillante, d'écarts imprévus, décevant l'oeil, le fouettant, l'irritant, le tenant en haleine par des lignes mille fois brisées se colorant par leurs brisures vibrantes dans les masses ondulatoires de l'atmosphère. . . . La lutte, l'hésitation, les conflits, la dé-

ception, la soif, tout ce qui constitue la vie doit constituer la vibration esthétique; de même que dans l'amour qu'on a pour une femme. Cela a été fait d'instinct dans les tableaux, la musique, la poésie. . . . La vie, la vie et encore rien que la vie, c'est-à-dire le nouveau." ("The ideal line is broken a thousand times, crackling with unforeseen disparities, deceiving the eye, lashing it, irritating it, holding it breathless by lines a thousand times broken being colored by their vibrating cracks in the undulating masses of the atmosphere. . . . Struggle, hesitation, conflicts, disappointments, and thirst, everything that makes up life ought to make up aesthetic vibration; just as in the love one has for a woman. That has been done instinctively in paintings, music and poetry. . . . Life, life and nothing but life, and by that I mean all that is new.")

35. *Mélanges Posthumes*, "Paysages et Impressions," pp. 32-33. ("A SPRING EVENING ALONG THE BOULEVARDS.—A spring evening on a bench, the great boulevards, near the Variétés. A café flooded with gas light. A floozy all in red going from beer-glass to beer-glass. On the second floor, quite somber, contemplative, lamps, tables, craniums bent low, a reading-room. On the third floor, the glow of the gas lamps, all the windows opened, flowers, scents, a dance. You don't hear the music in the loud uproar that comes up from the street swarming with pedestrians and taxis whose comings and goings devour and spit up the world without end and the program hawking in front of the Variétés.—But the length of these ten windows you see men dancing, in black tails, white shirt-fronts, turning in cadence, holding a blue-pink-lilac-white woman, holding her, hardly embracing her, very properly, you see them pass by, pass by again, serious, without laughing (you cannot hear the music that makes them dance). A group of pimps passes by; one says: 'Hey, she made ten francs.'—At the Variétés, the throng goes out for the intermission; and still the hell of the boulevard, the taxis, the cafés, the gas lights, the store windows, still the passers-by. These floozies who walk under the garish brightness of the cafés.—Near me a newspaper stand—two women are talking; one says: 'For certain, she won't last the night, and her brat who gave mine that mange.' Buses loaded with both sexes all having their emotional life, their troubles, their ruts.

"Overhead the sweet and eternal stars.")

36. *Les Nourritures Terrestres*, p. 21. ("Let the *importance* lie in your look, not in the thing you look at.")

37. Marcel Proust, *Oeuvres Complètes de Marcel Proust, Du Côté de chez Swann* (Paris: NRF Gallimard, 1929), p. 144. ("A little tap at the window, as though some missile had struck it, followed by a plentiful, falling sound, as light though; as if a shower of sand were

being sprinkled from a window overhead; then the fall spread, took on an order, a rhythm, became liquid, loud, drumming, musical, innumerable, universal. It was the rain.")

38. Rainer Maria Rilke, *Sämtliche Werke,* "Die Aufzeichnungen des Malte Laurids Brigge" (Frankfurt am Main: Inselverlag, 1966), pp. 716-717.

("Yes, for these absent-minded, drowsy things it was a terrible time. From books that some hasty hand had clumsily opened rose-leaves would tumble, to be trampled underfoot; small fragile objects were seized, and, when they were immediately broken, quickly put back again; many hidden things, too, were thrust beneath curtains, or even flung behind the gilt net-work of the fire-screen and from time to time something fell, fell muffled on carpeting, fell clear on the hard parquetry, but here and there it smashed, shattering sharply or cracking apart almost inaudibly, for these things, pampered as they were, could not survive any sort of fall.

"And had it occurred to anyone to ask what caused all this, what had called down upon this anxiously guarded room the full measure of destruction,–there would have been but *one* answer: Death.

"The death of Chamberlain Christoph Detlev Brigge at Ulsgaard.

. . .

"Christoph Detlev's death had been living at Ulsgaard for many, many days now and had spoken to everyone and demanded: demanded to be carried, demanded the blue room, demanded the little salon, demanded the large hall. Demanded the dogs, demanded that people should laugh, talk, play and be quiet and all at the same time. Demanded to see friends, women, and people who were dead, and demanded to die itself: demanded. Demanded and shouted.")

Conclusion

1. R.-M. Albérès, *Histoire du Roman Moderne.* (Paris: Albin Michel, 1962), p. 186. ("The reality of the novel is no longer in its surface, but in what it does not succeed in formulating completely.")

Bibliography

Bibliography

Albérès, René M. *L'Aventure Intellectuelle du XXe siècle*. Panorama des littératures européennes, 1900-1963. Paris: Albin Michel, 1959.

————. *Histoire du Roman Moderne*. Paris: Albin Michel, 1962.

————. *Métamorphoses du roman*. Paris: Albin Michel, 1966.

————. *Le roman d'aujourd'hui, 1960-1970* Paris: Albin Michel, 1970.

————. "Aux sources du nouveau roman: L'impressionnisme anglais," *Revue de Paris*, LXIX (May, 1962), 74-86.

Bahr, Hermann. *Expressionismus*. München: Delphin Verlag, 1918.

————. *Zur Überwindung des Naturalismus*. Theoretische Schriften 1887-1904. Stuttgart, Berlin, Köln, Mainz: Kohlhammer Verlag, 1968.

————. *Kulturprofile der Jahrhundertwende*. Wien: H. Bauer, 1962, pp. 176-186.

Balakian, Anna. *The Symbolist Movement*. A critical appraisal. New York: Random House, 1967.

Bally, Charles, *et al*. *El impresionismo en el lenguaje*. Buenos Aires: Universidad Nacional, 1936.

Balzac, Honoré de. *La Comédie Humaine*. IX, Etudes Philosophiques, I. Paris: Pleïade, Gallimard, 1950.

————. *Le Lys dans la Vallée*. Paris: Garnier Frères, 1966.

Batterby, K. A. *Rilke and France*. A Study in Poetic Development. London: Oxford University Press, 1966.

Baudelaire as a Literary Critic. Selected Essays, ed. Lois Boe Hyslop and Francis E. Hyslop, Jr. University Park: The Pennsylvania State University Press, 1964.

Baudelaire, Charles. *Oeuvres Complètes*. Paris: Pleïade, 1954.

Beach, Joseph Warren. *The Twentieth Century Novel*. New York: 1960.

Benamou, Michel. "Wallace Stevens: Some Relations between Poetry and Painting," *Comparative Literature*, II (1959), 47-60.

————. "Symposium on Literary Impressionism," *Yearbook of Comparative and General Literature*, No. 17 (1968), pp. 66 ff.

Bernard, Suzanne. "Rimbaud, Proust et les Impressionnistes," *Revue des Sciences Humaines*, LXXVIII (1955), 257-262.

Bithell, Jethro. *Modern German Literature*, 1880-1950. London: Methuen & Co., Ltd., 1959.

Bowie, Theodore Robert. *The Painter in French Fiction*, a critical essay. Chapel Hill: University of North Carolina, 1950.

Brunetière, Ferdinand. "L'impressionnisme dans le roman," *Le roman naturaliste*. Paris: Lévy, 1893.

Butor, Michel. *Les Oeuvres d'Art Imaginaires chez Proust*. University of London: The Athlone Press, 1964.

Chernowitz, Maurice. *Proust and Painting*. New York: International Universities Press, 1945.

Conrad, Joseph, *The Nigger of the "Narcissus,"* Preface. London: J. M. Dent and Sons, Ltd., 1897.

Dazai, Osamu. *No Longer Human*. New York: A New Directions Book, 1958.

Davis, Harold E. "Conrad's Revision of the Secret Agent: A Study in Literary Impressionism," *Modern Language Quarterly*, XIX (1958), 244-254.

De Nardis, Luigi. *Impressionismo di Mallarmé*. Rome: S. Sciascia, 1957.

Décaudin, Michel. "Poésie impressionniste et poésie symboliste," *Cahiers de l'Association Internationale des Études Françaises*, XII (1960), 132-142.

Decaves, Pierre. "Réalités du Roman," *La Table Ronde*, No. 157 (Janvier 1961), p. 165.

Desprez, L. *L'Evolution naturaliste*. Paris: Tresse, 1884, p. 94 ff.

Flaubert, Gustave. *L'Education Sentimentale*. Paris: Garnier Frères, 1964.

Francastel, Pierre. "La Fin de l'Impressionnisme: Esthétique et Causalité," in *Problems of the 19th and 20th Century Studies in Western Art*, IV. Princeton, N.J.: Princeton University Press, 1963.

————. *Peinture et Société*. Paris: NRF Gallimard, 1965.

Frank, Joseph. "Spatial Form in Literature," *Sewanee Review*, LIII (1945), 221-240; 433-456; 643-653.

Freedman, Ralph. *The Lyrical Novel*. Princeton, N.J.: Princeton University Press, 1963.

Geffroy, Gustave. "Salon de 1894," in *La Vie Artistique*. Paris: E. Dentu, 1895.

Gibbs, Beverly Jean. "Impressionism as a Literary Movement," *Modern Language Journal*, 36 (1952), 175-183.

Gide, André. *Les Cahiers et les Poésies d'André Walter*. Paris: NRF Gallimard, 1952.

————. *Les Faux-Monnayeurs*. Paris: Le Livre de Poche, 1925.

————. *The Journals of André Gide*, vol. III: 1928-1939. tr. Justin O'Brien. New York: Alfred A. Knopf, 1949.

————. *Les Nourritures Terrestres*. Paris: Le Livre de Poche, 1917-36.

Giraud, Raymond. *Flaubert*, a collection of critical essays. Englewood Cliffs, N.J.: Prentice-Hall, 1964.

Gourmont, Remy de. *Couleurs*. Paris: Mercure de France, 1920.

Hamann, Richard. *Der Impressionismus in Leben und Kunst*. Marburg: Kunstgeschichtliches Seminar, 1923.

Hatzfeld, Helmut. *Literature through Art*. New York: Oxford University Press, 1952.

————. *Trends and Styles in Twentieth Century French Literature*. Washington: Catholic University of America Press, 1957.

Hauser, Arnold. *The Social History of Art*, "Impressionism," vol. 4. New York: Vintage Books, 1951, pp. 166-225.

Hourticq, L. "Réalisme et Impressionnisme," in *L'Art et la Littérature*. Paris: Flammarion, 1946, pp. 217-259.

Howarth, Herbert. "Symposium in Literary Impressionism," *Yearbook of Comparative and General Literature*, No. 17, pp. 40-46.

Huyghe, René. "L'impressionnisme et la pensée de son temps," *Prométhée* (L'Amour de l'Art), I (Fév., 1939), pp. 7-16.

Ishikawa, Takéshi. *Etude sur la littérature impressionniste au Japon*. Paris: A Pedone, 1919.

Jácome, Benito Varela. *Renovacion de la novela en el siglo XX*. Barcelona: Ediciones Destino, 1966.

Joyce, James. *The Portable James Joyce*. New York: The Viking Press, 1958.

Julleville, L., Petit de. *Histoire de la Langue et de la Littérature Française*, des origines à 1900. Tome VIII, Paris: Armand Colin, 1899.

Kaelin, Eugene E. *An Existentialist Aesthetic*. The Theories of Sartre and Merleau-Ponty. Madison, Milwaukee, and London: The University of Wisconsin Press, 1966.

Keene, Donald. *Japanese Literature*. London: J. Murray, 1953.

Kronegger, Maria E. "The Theory of Unity and Effect in the Works of E. A. Poe and James Joyce," *Revue de Littérature Comparée*, 154 (Avril-Juin, 1965), 226-234.

————. "Impressionist Tendencies in Lyrical Prose," *Revue de Littérature Comparée*, 172 (Octobre-Décembre, 1969), 528-544.

Kumar, Shiv. *Bergson and the Stream of Consciousness Novel*. New York: New York University Press, 1962.

Laforgue, Jules. *Oeuvres Complètes. Mélanges Posthumes*. Critique d'Art. Paris: Mercure de France, 1903.

Lauterbach, Ulrich. *Hermann Bang*, Studien zum dänischen Impressionismus. Breslau: Maruschke & Berendt, 1937.

Lerch, Eugen. *Handbuch der Frankreichkunde*. "Die sinnliche Anschauungskraft (lebhafte Phantasie) der Franzosen und ihre sprachliche Spiegelung; der Impressionismus," vol. I. Frankfurt: Moritz Diesterweg, 1930, pp. 112-131.

Levin, Harry. *The Gates of Horn*: A Study of Five French Realists. "Flaubert." New York: Oxford University Press, 1966.

Lips, Marguerite. *Le Style indirect libre*. Paris: Payot, 1926.

Littré, Emile. *Dictionnaire de la langue française*. Paris: Hachette, 1962.

Loesch, Georg. "Die impressionistische Syntax der Goncourt. (Eine syntaktisch-stilistische Untersuchung)," Dissertation. Nürnberg: Benedikt Hilz, 1919.

Lombard, Alf. *Les Constructions nominales dans le Français moderne*, étude et stylistique. Uppsala et Stockholm: Almquist & Wiksell, 1933.

Lövgren, Sven. *The Genesis of Modernism*. Seurat, Gauguin, Van Gogh and French Symbolism in the 1880's. Stockholm: Almquist & Wiksell, 1958.

Mach, Ernst. *Contributions to the Analysis of Sensations*. Chicago: The Open Court Pub. Co., 1897.

Mallarmé, Stéphane. *Correspondance* 1862-1871, ed. Henri Mondor. Paris: NRF Gallimard, 1959.

Malraux, André. *Le Musée Imaginaire, Les Voix du Silence*. Paris: NRF Gallimard, ed. Idées/Arts, 1965.

Martin du Gard, Roger. *Recollections of André Gide*. New York: The Viking Press, 1953.

Marzynski, Georg. "Die impressionistische Methode," *Zeitschrift für Aesthetik und allgemeine Kunstwissenschaft*, XIV (1920), 90-94.

Mauclair, Camille. *Monet*. New York: Dodd, Mead & Co., 1924.

McClellan, Edwin. "The Impressionistic Tendency in some Modern Japanese Writers," *Chicago Review*, XVII, iv (1965), 48-60.

Melang, Walter. "Flaubert als Begründer des literarischen Impressionismus in Frankreich," Dissertation. Emsdetten: H. and J. Lechte, 1933.

Merleau-Ponty, Maurice. "Le doute de Cézanne," *Sens et Non-Sens*. Paris: Ed. Nagel, 1948.

————. *L'Oeil et l'Esprit*. Paris: NRF Gallimard, 1964.

Monnin-Hornung, Juliette. *Proust et la Peinture*. Geneva: E. Droz, 1951, pp. 102-136.

Morice, Charles. *Demain*. Questions d'Esthétique. Paris: Perrin, 1888.

Moser, Ruth. *L'Impressionnisme Français*: Peinture, Littérature, Musique. Geneva: E. Droz, 1952.

Mouton, Jean. "L'Optique de Proust, du regard à la vision," *Entretiens sur Marcel Proust* sous la direction de Georges Cattaui et Philip Kolb. Paris, La Haye: Mouton & Co., 1966, pp. 50-57.

Muller, Herbert J. *Modern Fiction. A Study of Values.* New York and London: Funk & Wagnalls Co., 1937.

————. "Impressionism in Fiction: Prism vs Mirror." *The American Scholar,* VII (1938), 355-367.

Nadal, Octave. *Paul Verlaine.* Paris: Mercure de France, 1961.

Niess, Robert J. *Zola, Cézanne, and Manet.* A Study of L'Oeuvre. Ann Arbor: University of Michigan Press, 1968.

Nochlin, Linda. *Impressionism and Post-Impressionism 1874-1904.* Sources and Documents. Englewood Cliffs, N.J.: Prentice-Hall, 1966.

Ortega y Gasset, José. *The Dehumanization of Art* and other writings on art and literature. Garden City, N.Y.: Doubleday Anchor Books, 1956.

Phillips, Duncan. *The Enchantment of Art.* New York: John Lane Co., 1914.

Poe, Edgar Allan. *Literary Criticism of Edgar Allan Poe,* ed. Robert L. Hough. Lincoln: University of Nebraska Press, 1965.

Praz, Mario. *Mnemosyne.* The parallel between literature and the visual arts. Princeton: Princeton University Press, 1970.

Proust, Marcel. *A la Recherche du Temps Perdu,* IV, A l'Ombre des Jeunes Filles en Fleurs, vol. 2. Paris: Gallimard, 1919.

————. *Oeuvres Complètes,* IX. *Du côté de chez Swann.* Paris: NRF, 1929.

————. *Oeuvres Complètes,* X. *Chroniques.* Paris: Gallimard, 1919.

————. *Les Plaisirs et les Jours.* Paris: NRF, Gallimard, 1924.

————. *Le Temps Retrouvé.* Paris: Le Livre de Poche, 1954.

————. *Swann's Way.* tr. C. K. Scott-Moncrieff. New York: Modern Library, 1956.

Rewald, John. *Cézanne,* sa vie, son ouèvre, son amitié pour Zola. Paris: Albin Michel, 1939.

————. *The History of Impressionism.* New York: The Museum of Modern Art, 1961.

Richard, Jean Pierre. *Littérature et Sensation.* Paris: Editions du Seuil, 1954.

Rilke, Rainer Maria. *Briefe über Cézanne.* Wiesbaden: Inselverlag, 1952.

————. "Les Cahiers de Malte Lauride Brigge" (Fragments) tr. A. Gide. *La Nouvelle Revue Française,* 1er julliet, 1911.

————. *Rodin.* London: The Grey Wall Press, 1946.

————. *Sämtliche Werke.* Sechster Band. "Die Aufzeichnungen des Malte Laurids Brigge." Frankfurt am Main: Inselverlag, 1966.

——————. *Selected Letters 1902-1926*, tr. F. C. Hull. London: Macmillan & Co., Ltd., 1947.

——————, et André Gide. *Correspondance 1909-1926*. Paris: Corréa, 1952.

——————, A. Gide et E. Verhaeren. *Correspondance inédite*. Paris: Ed. Messein, 1955.

——————. *Letters of Rainer Maria Rilke 1892-1910*. Tr. Jane Bannard Greene and M. D. Herter Norton. New York: W. W. Norton and Co., 1945.

Rimbaud. *Oeuvres*. Paris: Garnier, 1960.

Robbe-Grillet, Alain. *Pour le Nouveau Roman*. Paris: NRF Gallimard, 1963.

Rodin, Auguste. *L'Art*. Entretiens réunis par Paul Gsell. Paris: NRF, Gallimard, coll. Idées/Arts, 1957.

Sartre, Jean-Paul. *La Mort dans l'Ame*. Paris: Le Livre de Poche, Gallimard, 1949.

——————. *La Nausée*. Paris: Le Livre de Poche, 1938.

Serullaz, Maurice. *French Painting. The Impressionist Painters*. tr. W. J. Stracham. New York: Universe Books, Inc., 1960.

Signac, Paul. *D'Eugène Delacroix au Néo-impressionnisme*. Paris: Floury, 1939.

Simon, Claude. *L'Herbe*. Paris: Editions de Minuit, 1958.

——————. "Claude Simon, franc-tireur de la révolution romanesque," an interview by Thérèse de Saint Phalle, in *Le Figaro Littéraire* (le 6 avril 1967).

Simon, Pierre Henri. *Théâtre Destin*. La signification de la renaissance dramatique en France au XXe siècle. Paris: Librairie Armand Colin, 1959.

Sommerhalder, Hugo. *Zum Begriff des literarischen Impressionismus*. Zürich: Poligraphischer Verlag, 1961.

Spitzer, Leo. *Stilstudien*, I, II. München: Max Hueber Verlag, 1961.

Sypher, Wylie. *Rococo to Cubism in Art and Literature*. Transformations in Style, in Art and Literature from the 18th to the 20th Century. New York: Vintage, 1960.

Ullmann, Stephen. *Style in the French Novel*. Cambridge: The University Press, 1957.

Venturi, Lionello. *Painting and Painters*. How to look at a picture, from Giotto to Chagall. New York: Charles Scribner's Sons, 1945.

——————. "The Aesthetic Idea of Impressionism," *The Journal of Aesthetics and Art Criticism*. New York: The Philosophical Library, No. 1 (Spring, 1941), pp. 34-45.

——————. *Les Archives de l'Impressionnisme*. Paris, New York: Durand-Ruel, 1939.

Weisbach, Werner. *Impressionismus.* Ein Problem der Malerei in der Antike und Neuzeit. Berlin: G. Grote'sche Verlagsbuchhandlung, 1919.

Wellek, René, and Austin Warren. *Theory of Literature.* New York: A Harvest Book, Harcourt, Brace & World, Inc., 1956.

Winner, Viola Hopkins. *Henry James and the Visual Arts.* Charlottesville: The University Press of Virginia, 1970.

Zola, Emile. *Salons,* recueillis, annotés et présentés par F. W. J. Hemmings et Robert J. Niess. Genève: E. Droz, 1959.

Index

Index

D'Annunzio, Gabriele, 32
Antonioni, Michelangelo, 80-81
Azorin, José Martinez Ruiz, 32

Balzac, Honoré, 24, 25, 26, 30, 31, 64, 70-71
Barrès, Maurice, 63
Baudelaire, Charles, 15, 18, 19, 27, 28, 30, 32, 47, 52, 60, 64, 70, 82, 89, 129, 132
Bazille, Frédéric, 30
Bergson, Henri, 87
Brunetière, Ferdinand, 24
Butor, Michel, 14, 32

Cézanne, Paul, 18, 19, 30, 31, 38, 110-11, 130
Chekhov, Anton, 32, 118
Chevreul, Eugène, 27, 129
classicism, 24
Conrad, Joseph, 30, 32, 37, 39
Corot, Camille, 52
Courbet, Gustave, 80
Crane, Stephen, 32

Dazai, Osamu, 13, 19-20, 28, 29, 32, 53, 56-57, 61, 66
Debussy, Claude, 15, 32, 46, 70, 80
decadent, 24, 30
Degas, Edgar, 38, 77, 106-7, 115, 120
Delacroix, Eugène, 33, 70, 92-93
Descartes, René, 87
Dilthey, William, 60
Dos Passos, John, 32

expressionism, 28-29

Faulkner, William, 32
Fauré, Gabriel, 70
Flaubert, Gustave, 13, 15, 16, 17, 18, 21, 25, 28, 29, 31, 43, 44, 48, 49, 51, 53, 54, 61, 62, 63, 66, 72-73, 78, 81, 89, 135
Fletcher, John Gould, 32, 122
Forster, E. M., 32

Gauguin, Paul, 130
George, Stephan, 32
Gide, André, 13, 15, 16, 17, 18, 21, 28, 32, 35, 39, 43, 44-46, 47, 49, 52, 53, 58, 60-61, 64-65, 66, 74, 84, 88, 89
Giraudoux, Jean, 72
Goethe, Johann Wolfgang von, 129
Goncourts, Edmund and Jules, 25, 29, 31, 51, 132
Gourmont, Remy de, 132

Helmholtz, Hermann von, 27
Hofmannsthal, Hugo von, 32
Hueffer, F. Madox, 32

illusionism, 30, 121
imagism, 24

James, Henry, 30, 32, 48
Jongkind, Johann Barthold, 130
Joyce, James, 28, 29, 32, 41, 48, 52, 76, 78, 85

Kafka, Franz, 26
Kant, Emmanuel, 14, 42

Laforgue, Jules, 14, 32, 39, 82-83, 89, 137
Lanier, Sidney, 122
Lawrence, David Herbert, 30, 32
Liebermann, Max, 30
la ligne brisée, 83
Liliencron, Detlev von, 32
Lowell, Amy, 32

153

Mach, Ernst, 13, 48
Mallarmé, Stéphane, 32, 64, 70, 77, 89
Manet, Edouard, 115, 130, 137
Mansfield, Katherine, 32, 48
Martin du Gard, Roger, 54
Memling, Hans, 59
Merleau-Ponty, Maurice, 13, 14, 20, 38, 77
Metzys, Quentin, 59
Miró, Joan, 32
mise en abyme, 11, 17, 58-59
modernism, 24
Molière, Jean-B., 64
Monet, Claude, 23, 30, 38, 43, 44, 46, 69, 70, 100-5, 120, 122, 130, 136, 137
Moore, George, 32
Morisot, Berthe, 30
Musil, Robert, 26

naturalism, 24, 25, 31, 36, 53
Nietzsche, Friedrich, 46, 87
nouveau roman, 28

Ortega y Gasset, José, 52, 81

Pater, Walter, 23
phenomenology, 13, 14, 17, 20, 25, 26, 38, 41, 42
Pissarro, Camille, 30, 44, 69, 96-97, 137
Poe, Edgar Allan, 32, 58, 63, 70, 71-72, 77, 82, 85, 87
Pound, Ezra, 48
Proust, Marcel, 13, 14, 15, 16, 17, 26, 32, 36, 39, 41, 48, 49, 52, 53, 54-55, 58, 64, 69, 73, 74, 76, 82, 84, 88, 118, 135

Racine, Jean, 121
realism, 14, 24, 25, 36
Renoir, Auguste, 30, 38, 45, 60, 81, 83, 98-99, 122, 130, 137
Rilke, Rainer Maria, 13, 15, 18, 19, 28, 29, 30, 31, 32, 53, 61, 62, 64, 65, 66, 67, 84, 87
Rimbaud, Arthur, 15, 27, 29, 32, 52, 63, 64, 77, 81, 82, 89
Robbe-Grillet, Alain, 13, 17, 20, 21, 32, 41, 49, 53, 57, 76, 89
Rodenbach, Georges, 32
Rodin, Auguste, 18, 30, 66
roman artistique, 26
roman phénoménologique, 26
romanticism, 25, 38, 71

Saltus, Edgar, 122
Sarraute, Nathalie, 21, 32, 41, 89
Sartre, Jean-Paul, 13, 20, 28, 40, 51-53, 55-56, 61, 62, 63, 64, 66, 77, 78, 79, 88, 89
Schopenhauer, Arthur, 37
Seurat, George, 38, 130
Signac, Paul, 30, 33
Simon, Claude, 13, 17, 20, 41, 57-58, 76, 89
Stein, Gertrude, 32
Stendhal, Henri (Beyle), 25
style sténographique, 128
surrealist, 29
Swinburne, Charles, 32
symbolism, 24, 25, 27, 36

Turner, William, 129

Van Gogh, Vincent, 29, 108-9, 130
Verhaeren, Emile, 32
Verlaine, Paul, 15, 32, 88, 89, 132, 137
Vermeer de Delft, Jean, 30

Whistler, James, 80, 82, 94-95
Whitman, Walt, 32
Wilde, Oscar, 32, 122
Woolf, Virginia, 26, 28, 32, 41

Yeats, William Butler, 39

Zola, Emile, 24, 25, 31, 37, 42